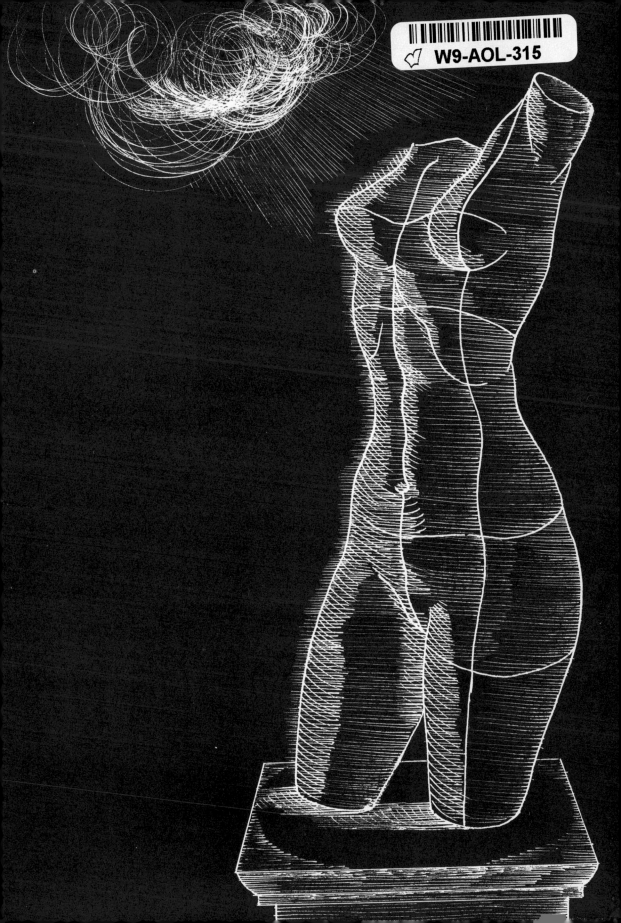

Pictorial Anatomy of the Human Figure

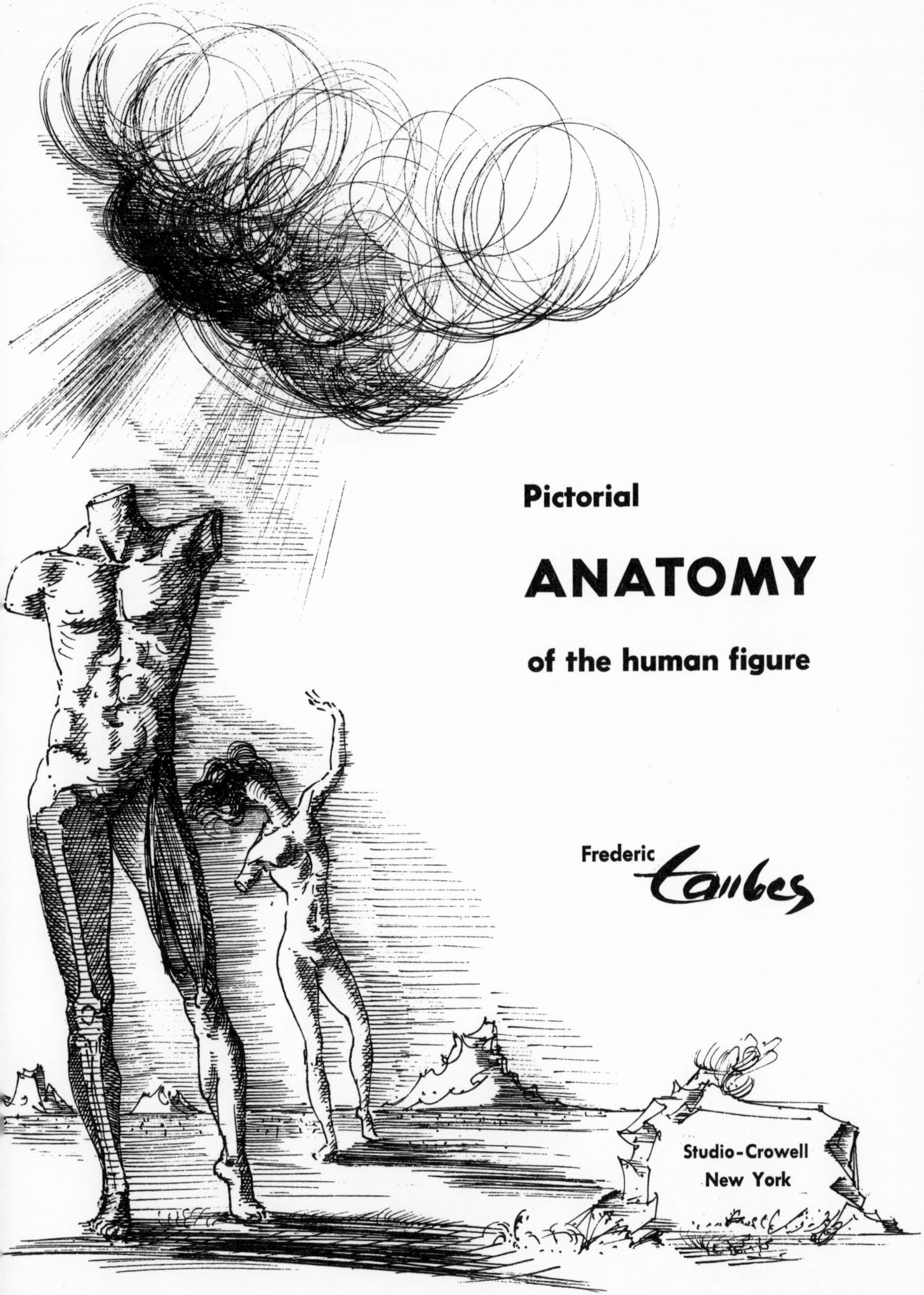

Pictorial

ANATOMY

of the human figure

Frederic Taubes

Studio-Crowell
New York

Designed by EMIL SILVESTRI

LIBRARY OF CONGRESS CATALOG CARD NO. 56-6238

Manufactured in the United States of America

Pictorial Anatomy of the Human Figure

PREFACE

In the course of years, countless
books on anatomy have been written. Some of them
touch the outer surface in one fashion or another,
some are skin deep, some go as deep as the
bones, even the marrow. The question arises: Of all
the expositions — detailed or sketchy — what
is of practical use for the contemporary painter?
I say "contemporary painter" advisedly, for
the discipline of anatomy means different things to us
from what it meant to the men who
established the science five centuries
ago. To the early Renaissance masters, the pursuit
of studies in the field of anatomy — and perspective
as well — was a creative act. Charting the
course of every muscle and sinew and discovering its
function was of great importance to these
masters; it is not of the same
concern to us, at least not to the painter.
          The practicing painter's needs as
regards the knowledge of anatomy — expressed
in a detailed catalogue of outer and
inner muscles and bones — are comparatively limited.
This is not to say that an excess of
knowledge could handicap or could even be
harmful to anyone, unless the student got to the
point that he couldn't see the

woods for the trees.

It is common experience that flayed
bodies such as are depicted in anatomical
books have, with regard to muscular appearance,
little semblance to living models, especially females;
and, among men, only trained athletes
would evidence the "ideal" physique. Besides, bodies
stressing muscularity have hardly a place
in the art of our time except as
illustrations for medical journals.
Nevertheless anatomy is most important to the painter,
and there is no book that I know of that
gives him what he really needs.
With this in mind, I have scaled down the great
mass of anatomical information to main
characteristics that are of practical use to the painter.
I have presented this reference material in an
informal sketchbook manner, for the most part, adding
spot illustrations which I believe
make each exposition more entertaining.
At one time the study of anatomy was
one of my cherished preoccupations.
Early in my art studies I became acquainted
with practically all the important phases of the subject,
and in the end I could draw even a single
vertebra — from memory. Since then
I found it useful to forget many of these
"facts" in order to approach
the subject with a contemporary eye.
I have endeavored, whenever possible,
to avoid Latin terms, because,
when used by a nonprofessional, the scientific
language of the medical men acquires,
more often than not, a ludicrous tinge, for it suggests
a familiarity with a science totally
foreign to the painter, to the orbit of
his comprehension. The same reasons compelled me to
reduce the text to captions only.
It is my contention that hardly any painter
could read a scientific text without

getting helplessly lost in a welter of medical
technicalities. With a great economy of means
I have attempted to present the physical
quality of the human figure in such a way as to give
the student an adequate understanding of the problems
of anatomy, in so far as it relates to the
problem of the painter of today.

Human bodies, mechanically and in
point of articulation, are obviously built on
the same principles. However, as we know, they
are quite dissimilar in outward appearance. And I do
not mean dissimilar only regarding proportions
and the skeletal build, but regarding
the topography of their surfaces.
Depending on the circumstance of muscle
development — or nondevelopment — and the
vagaries of the distribution of fatty tissues, we may
at times find ourselves at odds with "facts"
known from precedents when we face a
body that does not seem to conform to such facts.

Hence, in treating the subject of
pictorial anatomy in this book I shall, whenever
appropriate, start with a general demonstration
of human anatomy in formalized manner. Once a human form
becomes part of one's residual memory — a
conceptual certainty, so to speak — we shall not
easily go astray in drawing or painting it
even without the aid of a model.
No two ears are alike; their intricacies
are such that the student may at times lose
his way among the declivities, hillocks, and ridges
of their surface. In establishing a schematic
representation of a universal ear, neck, thigh, etc.,
as it were, I have attempted to help the
student in a better understanding
of the characteristic forms underlying the
structure, sometimes to the point of exaggeration,
which will emphasize or dramatize a shape and
give it vitality that would be lacking
in an overdetailed exposition.

The surface contours

Heads in "lost" profile
and in foreshortened position

After Leonardo

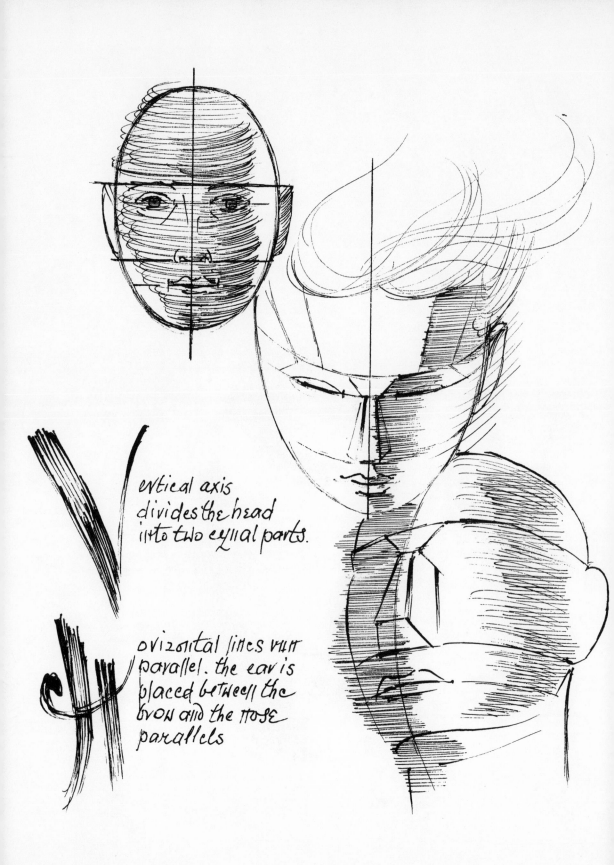

ertical axis
divides the head
into two equal parts.

orizontal lines run
parallel. the ear is
placed between the
brow and the nose
parallels

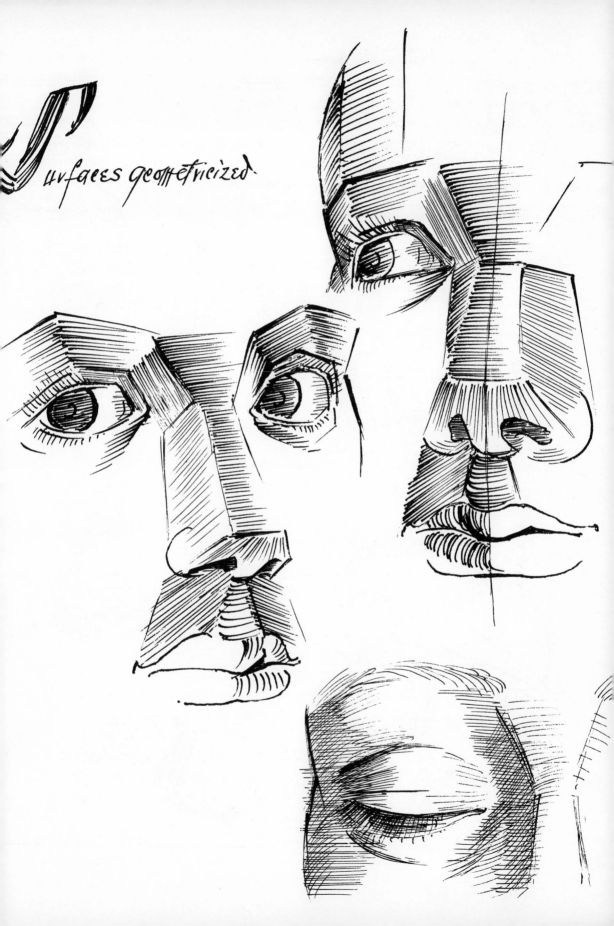

urfaces geometricized.

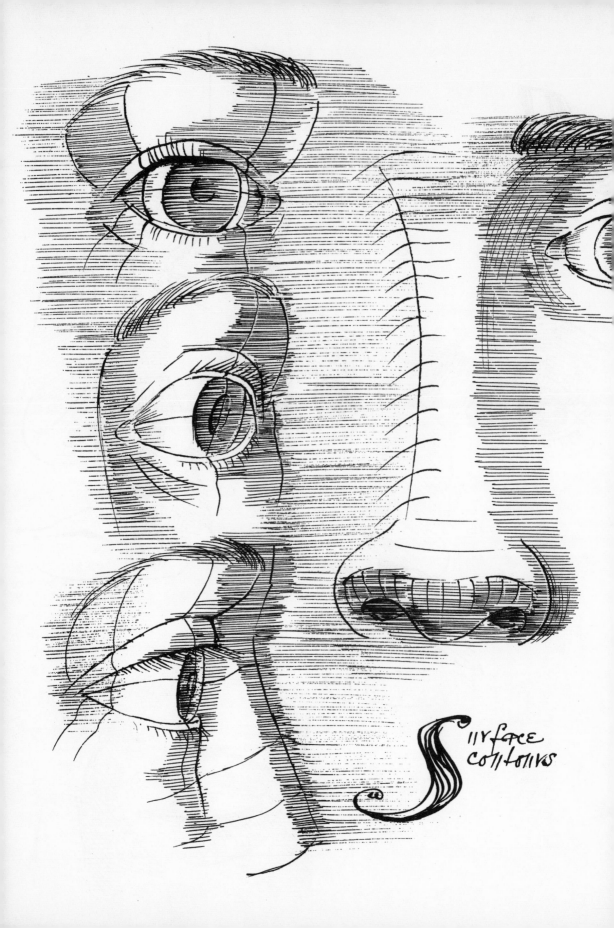

surface
contours

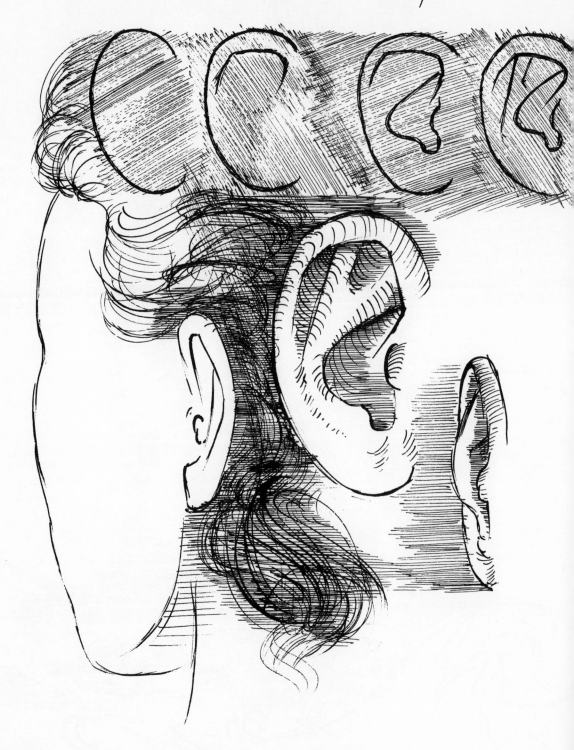

the NECK

the characteristic
shape of the neck is
formed by the position
of sternomastoids atta-
ched behind the ear
and terminating bet-
ween the collarbones
where they meet at a
U form at the head
of the breastbone.

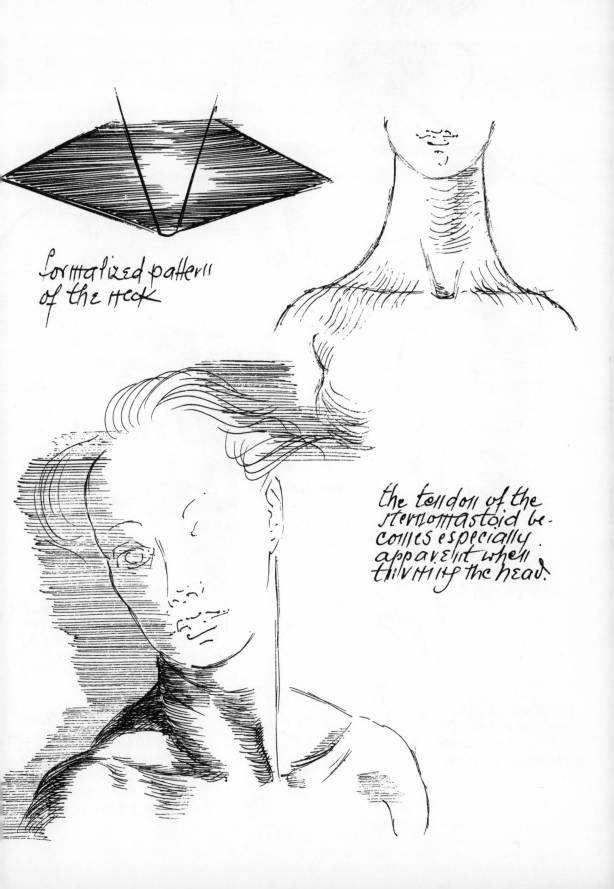

formalized pattern
of the neck

the tendon of the
sternomastoid be-
comes especially
apparent when
turning the head.

sternomastoid

hood muscle
(trapezius)

E

junction of the
shoulder blade (D)
and the collarbone
(acromion process)

D

C

the collarbone is
visible under the skin
in the area between
the breastbone (A)
the hood muscle (B),
and the deltoid (C)

the seventh vertebra
of the neck (E) ap-
pears prominently
on the spine; it divi-
des the neck from
the shoulder

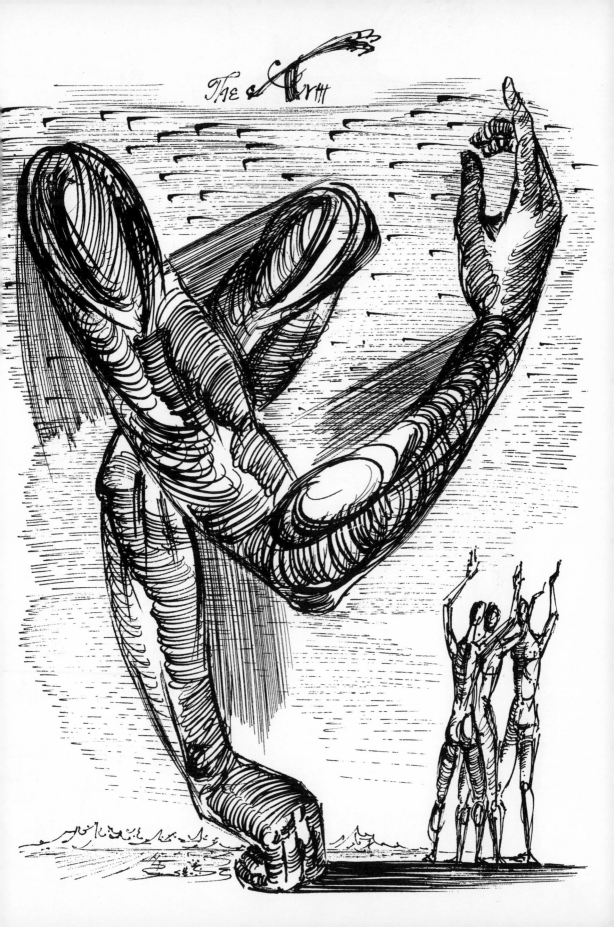

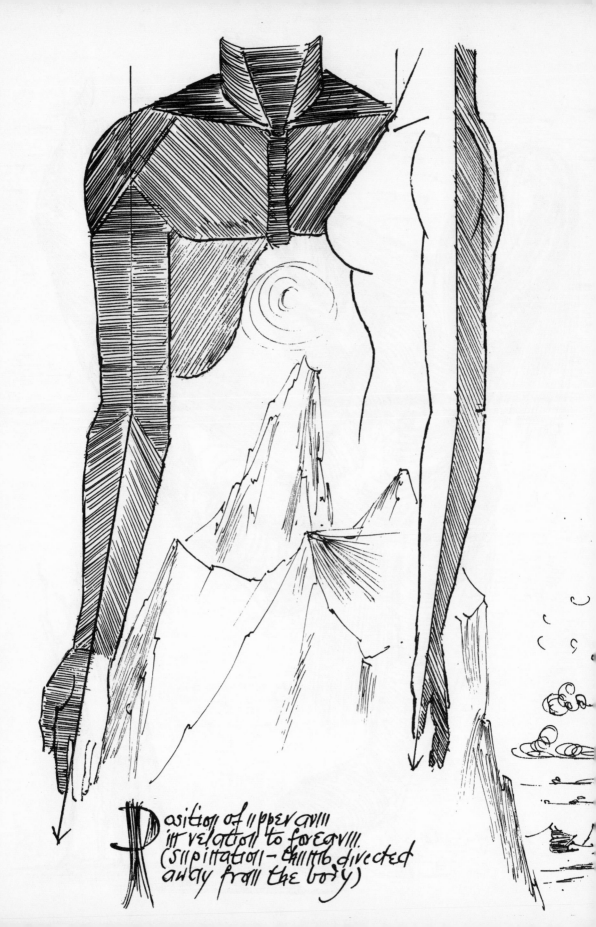

Position of upper arm
in relation to forearm.
(supination - thumb directed
away from the body)

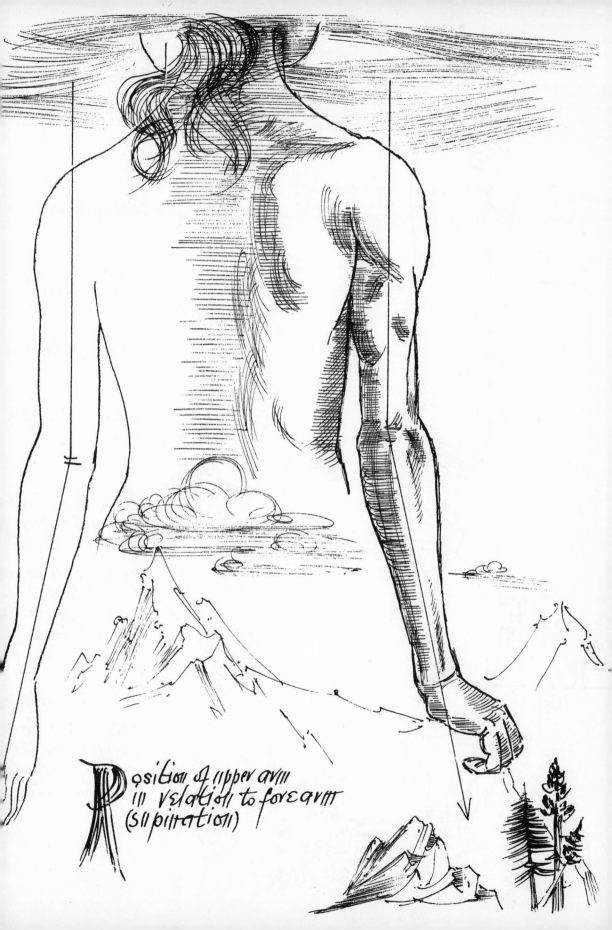

Position of upper arm
in relation to forearm
(supination)

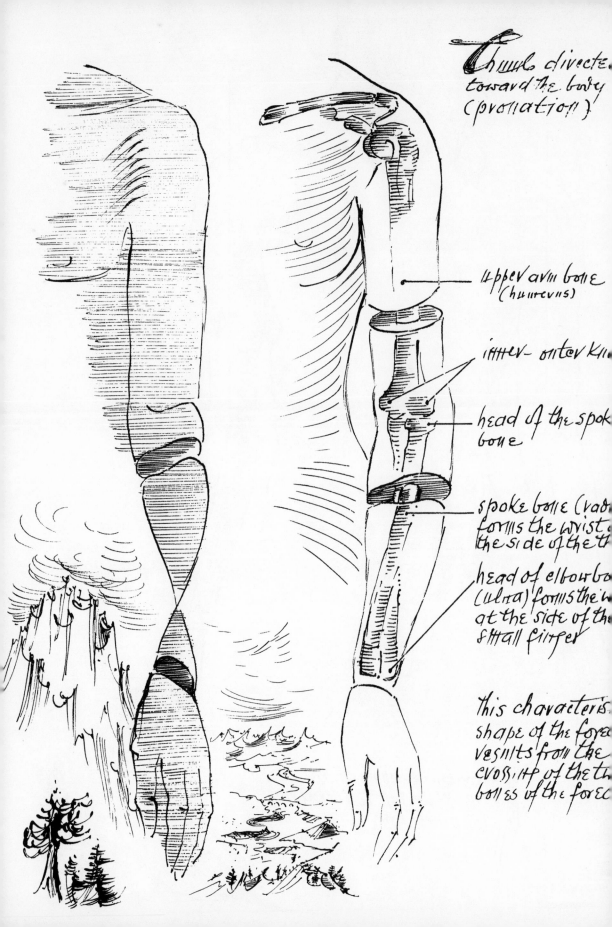

thumb directed
toward the body
(pronation)

upper arm bone
(humerus)

inner-outer knu...

head of the spok...
bone

spoke bone (rad...
forms the wrist...
the side of the th...

head of elbow bo...
(ulna) forms the w...
at the side of the
small finger

this characteris...
shape of the fore...
results from the
crossing of the tw...
bones of the forea...

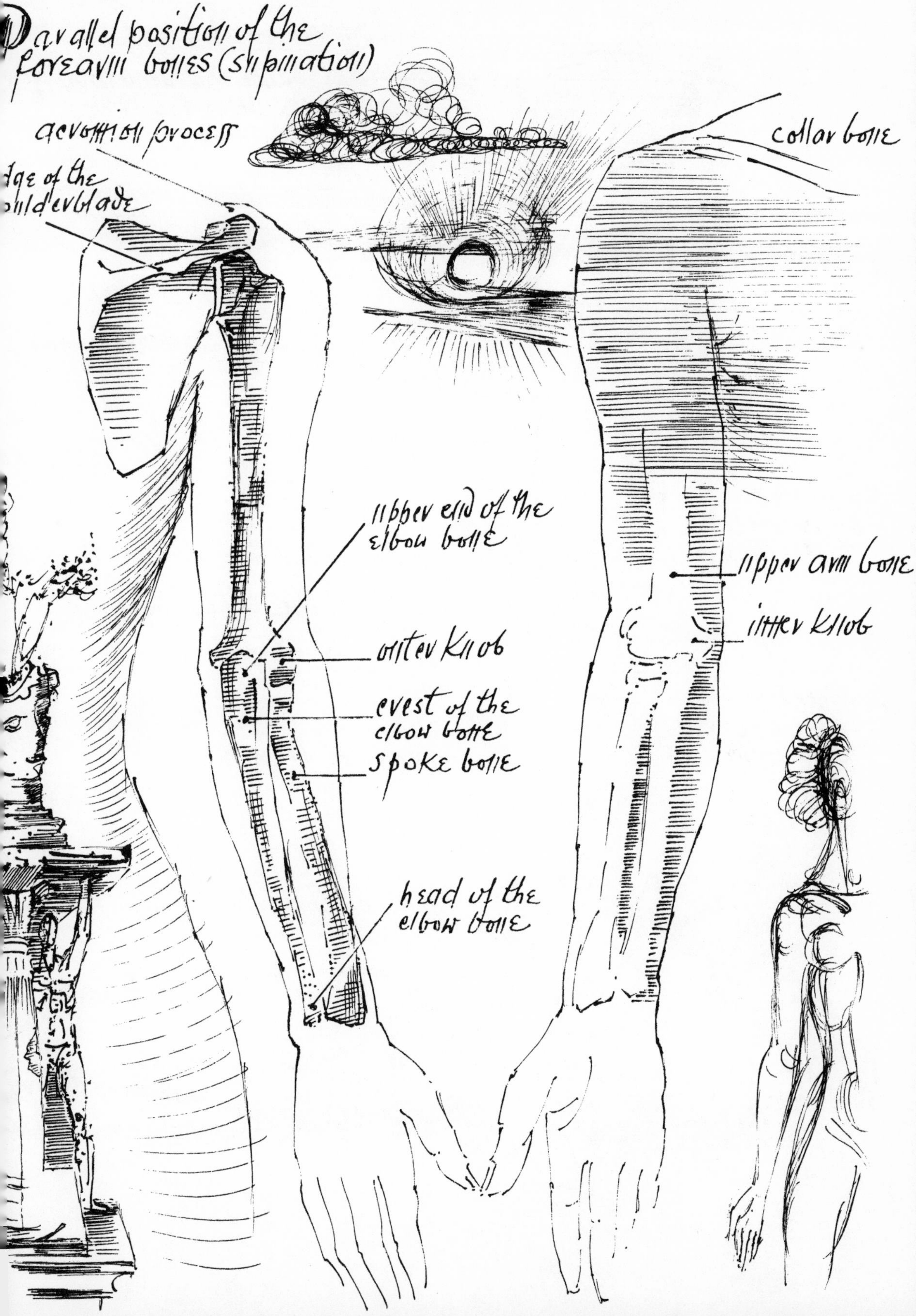

Parallel position of the forearm bones (supination)

acromion process

edge of the shoulderblade

collar bone

upper end of the elbow bone

upper arm bone

outer knob

inner knob

crest of the elbow bone

spoke bone

head of the elbow bone

hood muscle (trapezius)

the ridge of the shoulder blade mark
its presence under the skin

deltoid

triceps

furrow formed by the outer head of
the triceps

shallow area of the tendon

muscles
belonging to the
triceps group

crest of the elbow bone

group of EXTENSORS

inner knob
of the upper
arm bone

group of flexors

head of the elbow bone

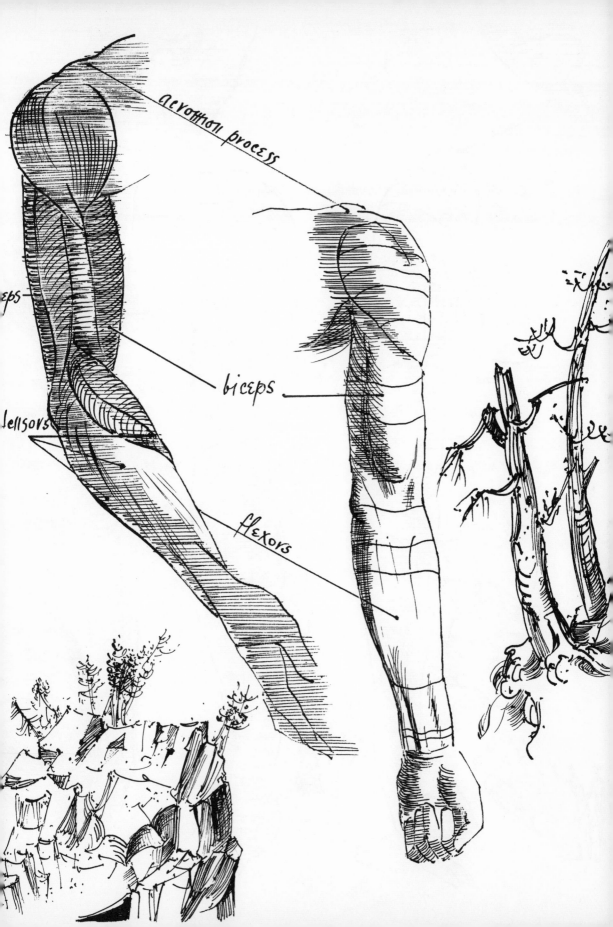

acromion process

eps

biceps

tensors

flexors

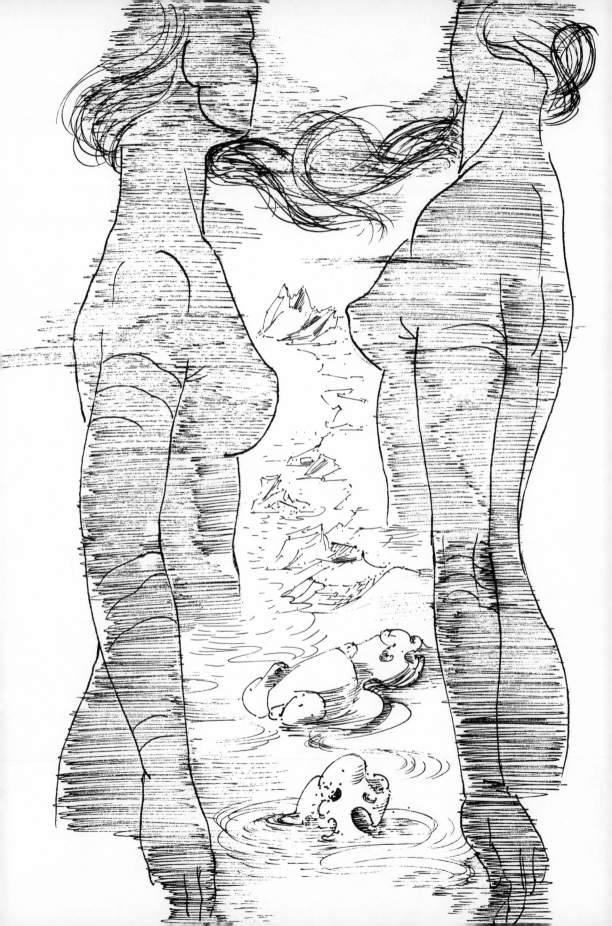

the E lbow (right arm)

back view   side view

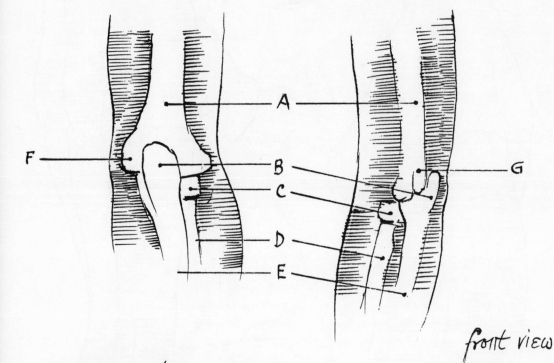

A
F
B
C
D
E
G

front view

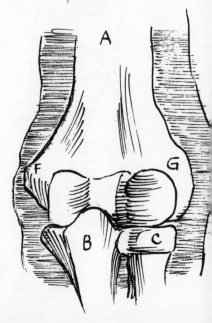

A upper arm bone
B upper end of the elbow bone
c head of the spoke bone
D spoke bone
E elbow bone
F inner knob
G outer knob

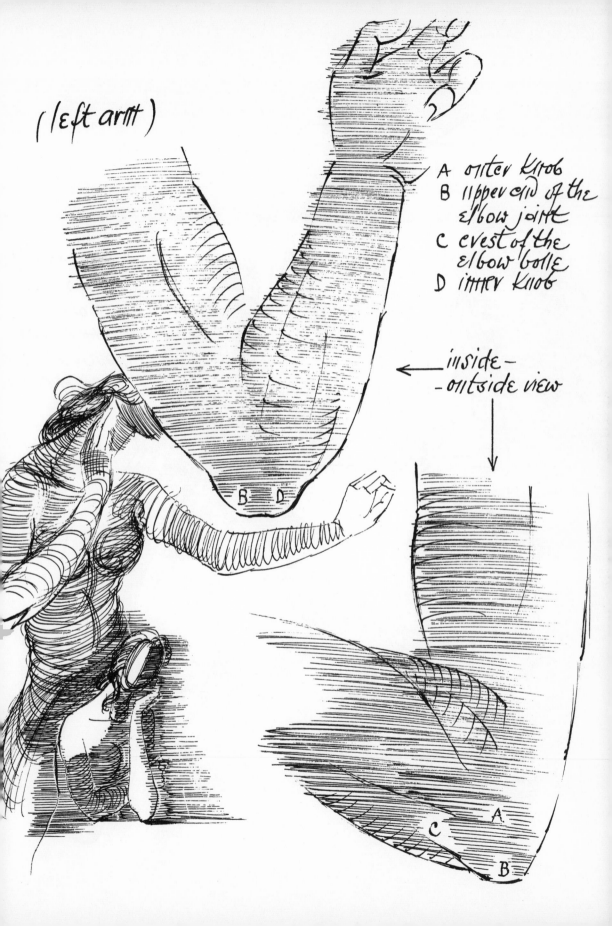

(left arm)

A outer knob
B upper end of the
   elbow joint
C crest of the
   elbow bone
D inner knob

inside-
-outside view

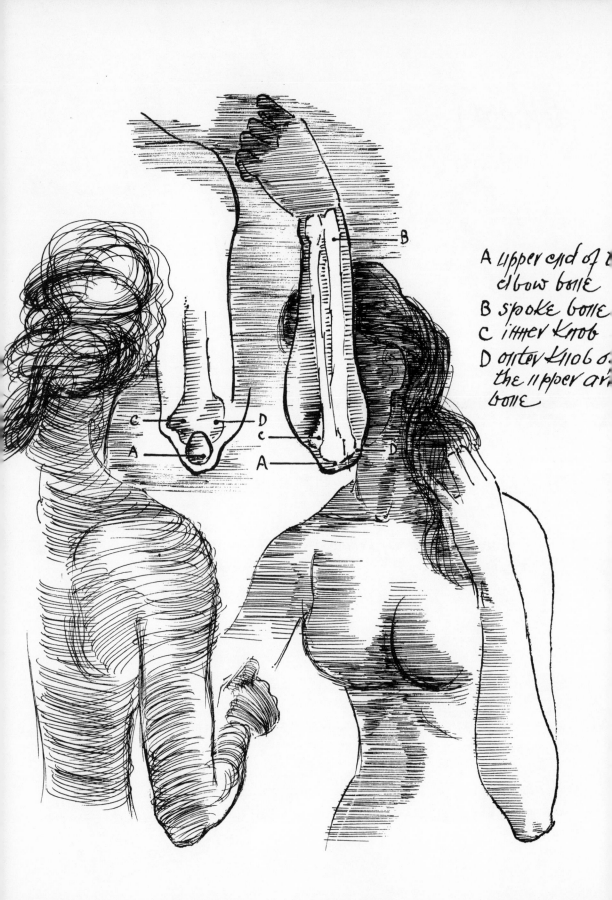

A upper end of the elbow bone

B spoke bone

C inner knob

D outer knob of the upper arm bone

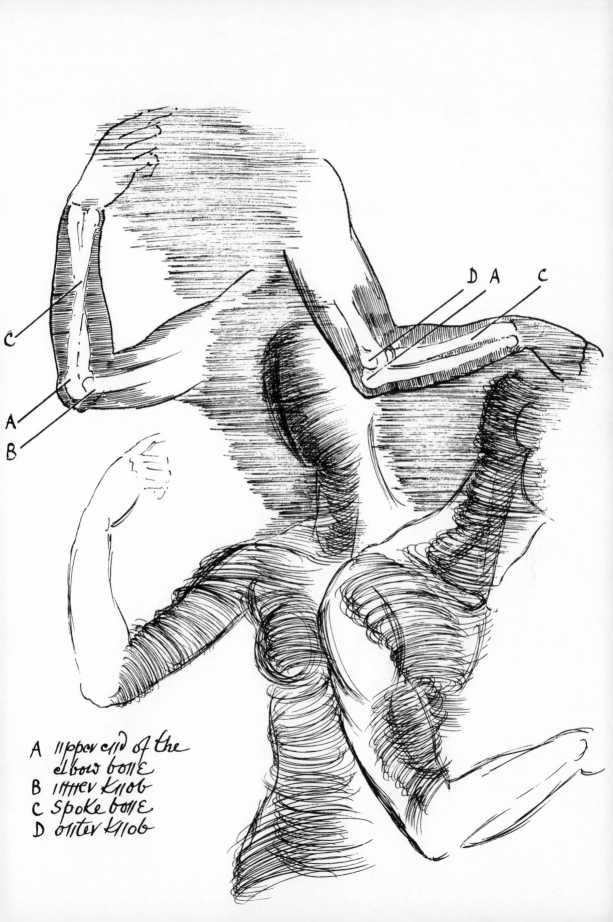

A upper end of the elbow bone
B inner knob
C spoke bone
D outer knob

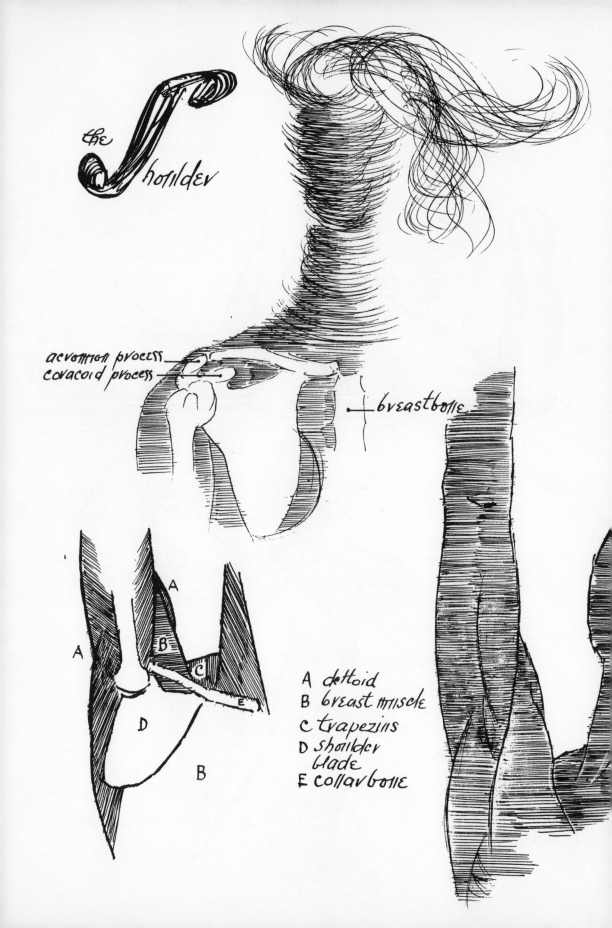

the Shoulder

acromion process
coracoid process

breastbone

A deltoid
B breast muscle
c trapezius
D shoulder
   blade
E collarbone

The She

the **S**houlder-blades

the inner border and the ridge of the shoulderblade (R.) shape the upper part of the back.

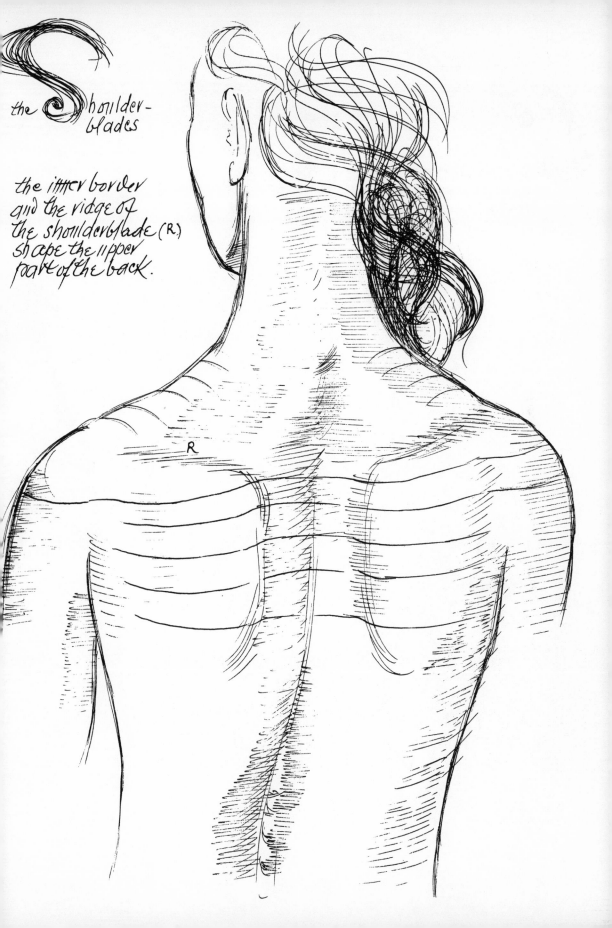

Collarbone and
shoulderblade

A acromion process
B collarbone

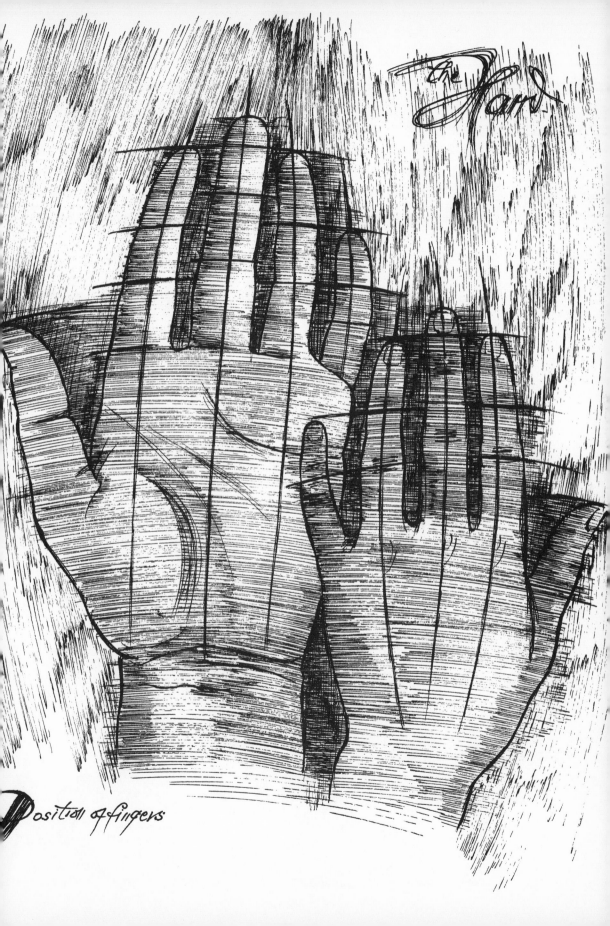

The Hand

Position of fingers

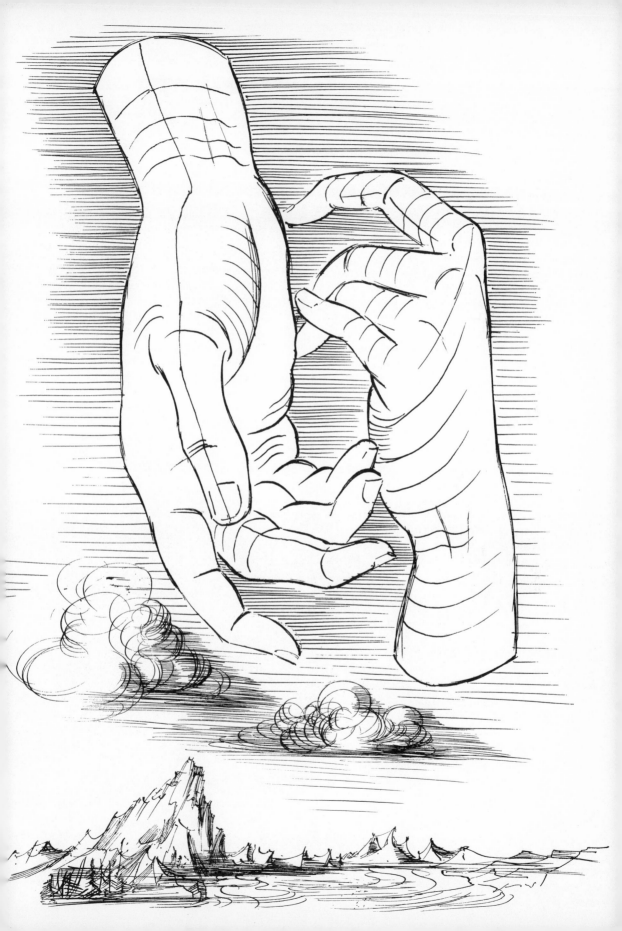

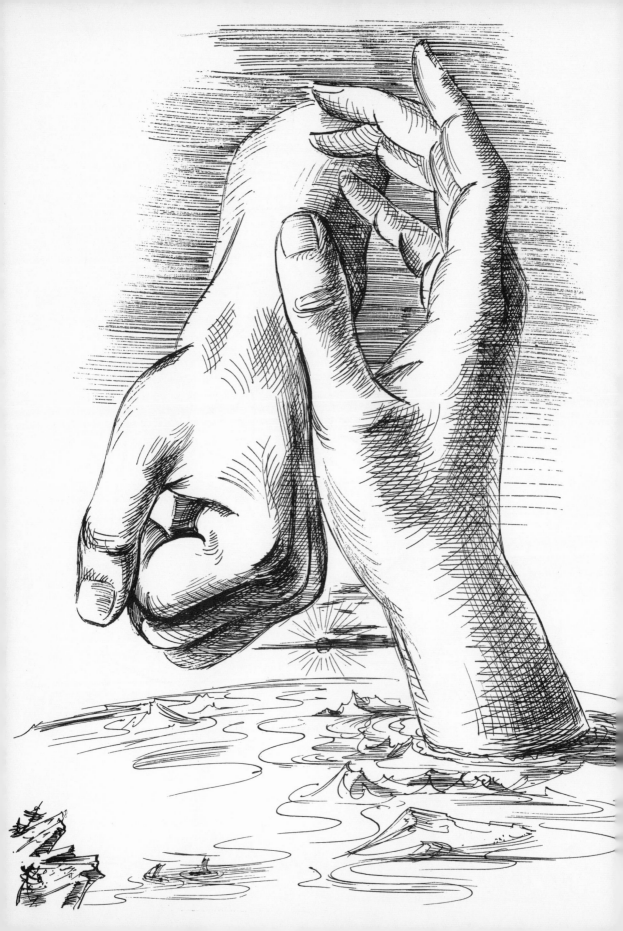

chematic representation

the tailor's muscle (A-B) divides
the thigh into two characteristic
shapes, but as such it is not visible
on the body. It starts at the edge
of the pelvis (crest of the ilium)
and terminates at the inner side
of the knee. — the outer contour
of the leg forms two convex contours; the inner, four convex contours.

A

B

1

2

1

2

3

4

2

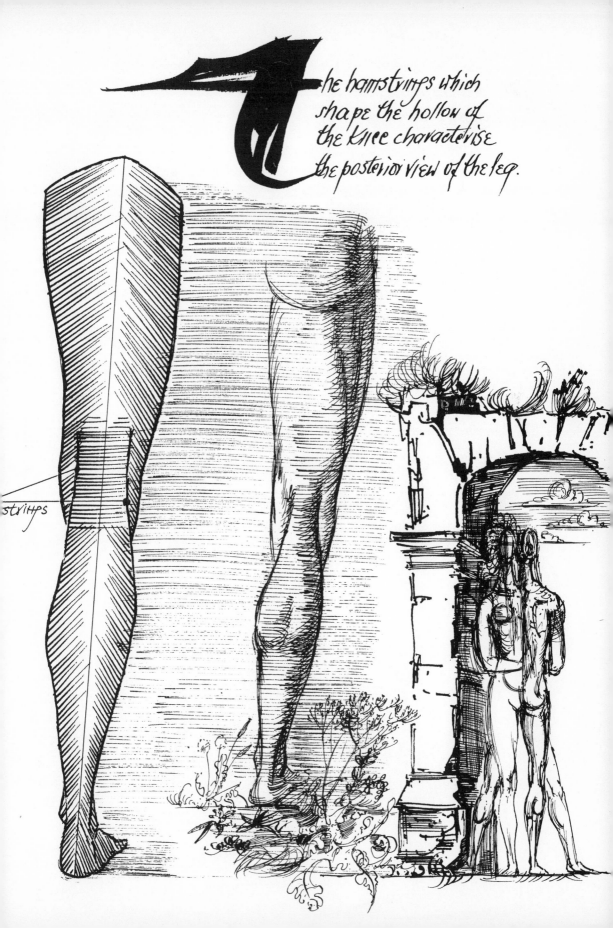

The hamstrings which shape the hollow of the knee characterise the posterior view of the leg.

STRIHPS

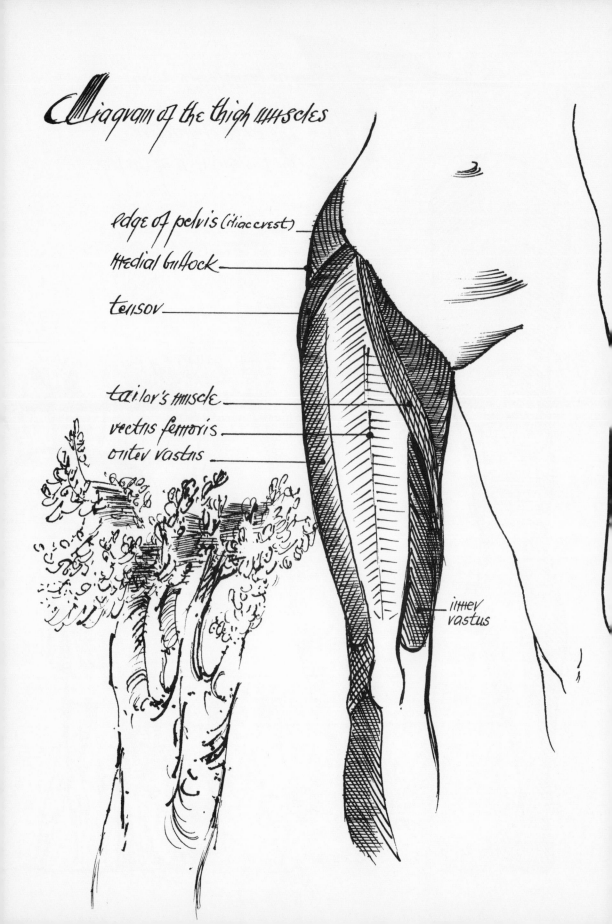

Diagram of the thigh muscles

edge of pelvis (iliac crest)

Medial buttock

tensor

tailor's muscle

rectus femoris

outer vastus

inner vastus

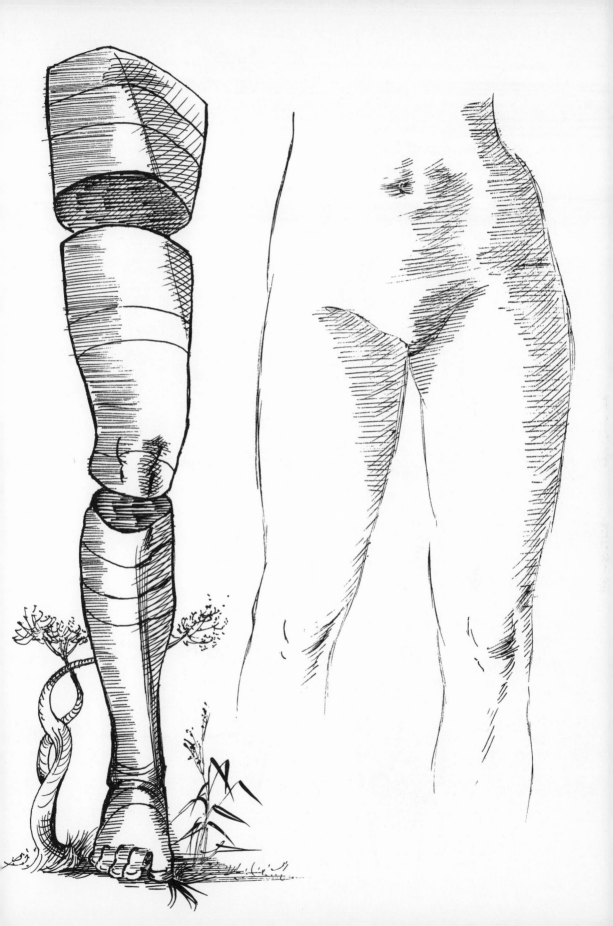

Thigh and Buttock

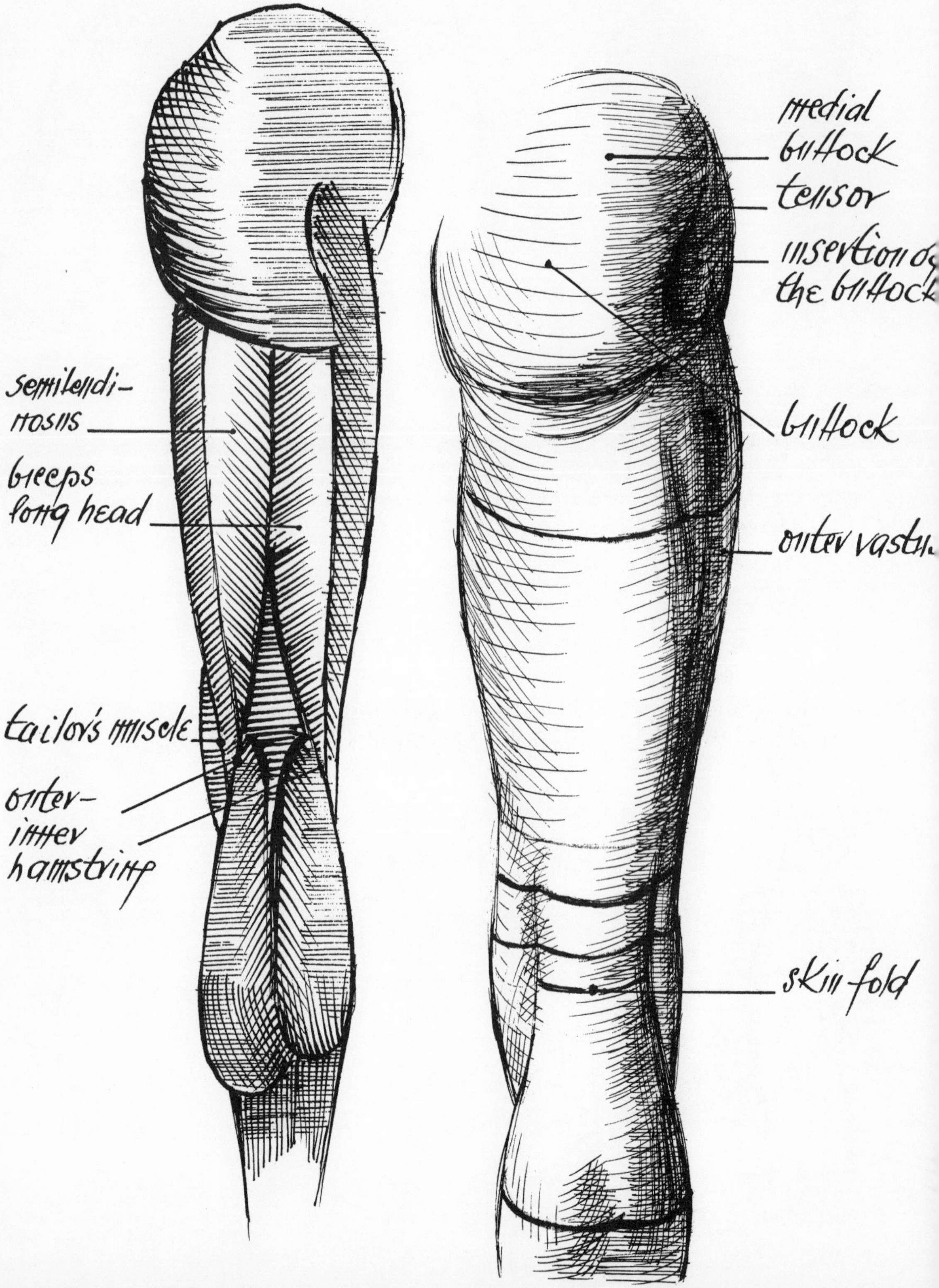

medial
buttock
tensor

insertion of
the buttock

semitendi-
nosus

biceps
long head

buttock

outer vastus

tailor's muscle

outer-
inner
hamstring

skin fold

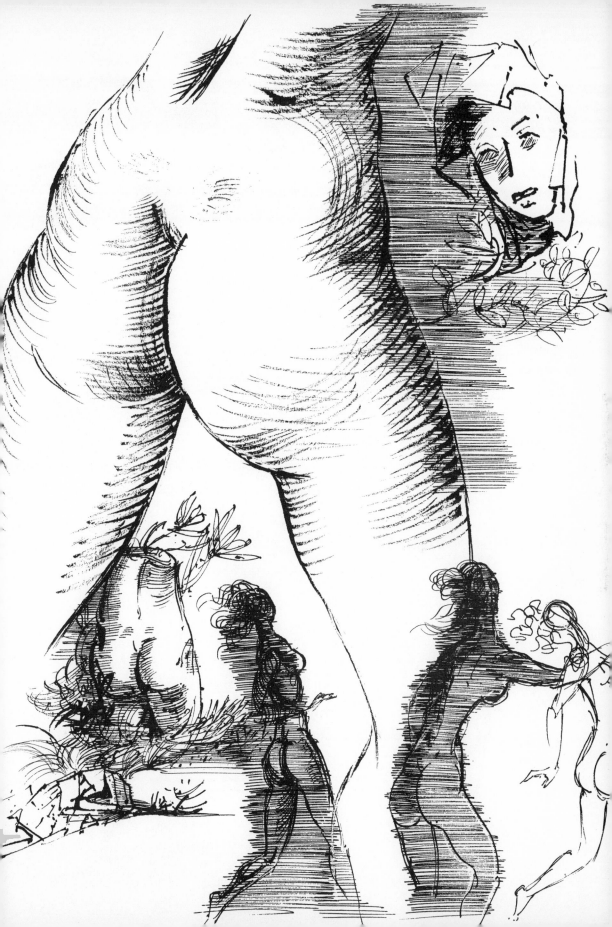

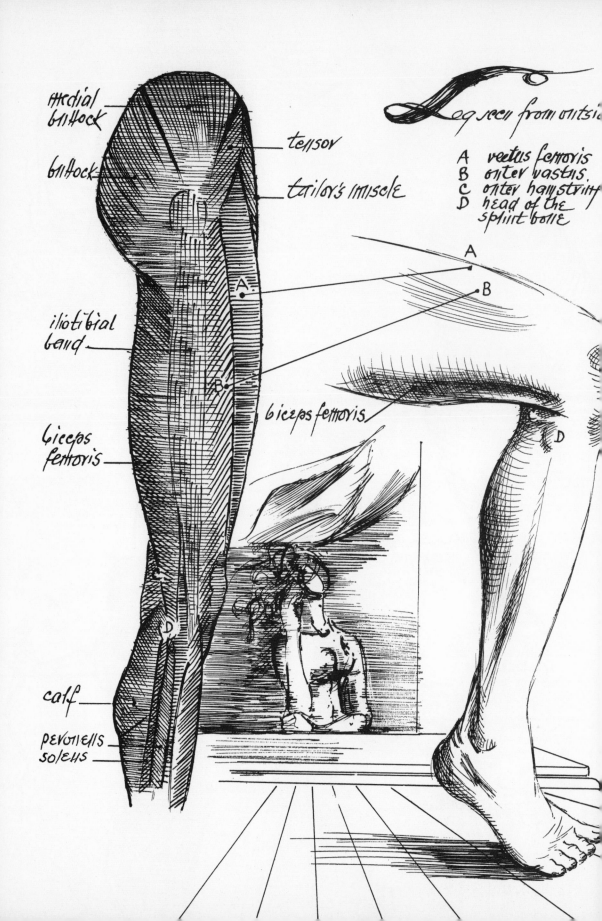

medial buttock

buttock

tensor

tailor's muscle

Leg seen from outside

A vestus femoris
B outer vastus.
C outer hamstring
D head of the splint bone

A

B

iliotibial band

biceps femoris

B

biceps femoris

D

calf

peronells
soleus

D

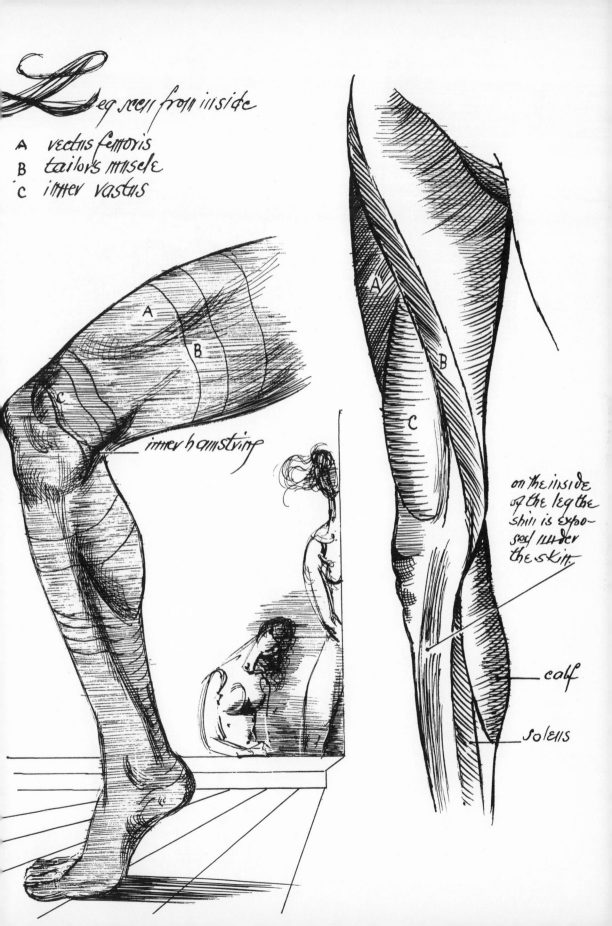

Leg seen from inside

A vectus femoris
B tailors muscle
C inner vastus

inner hamstring

on the inside of the leg the shin is exposed under the skin.

calf

soleus

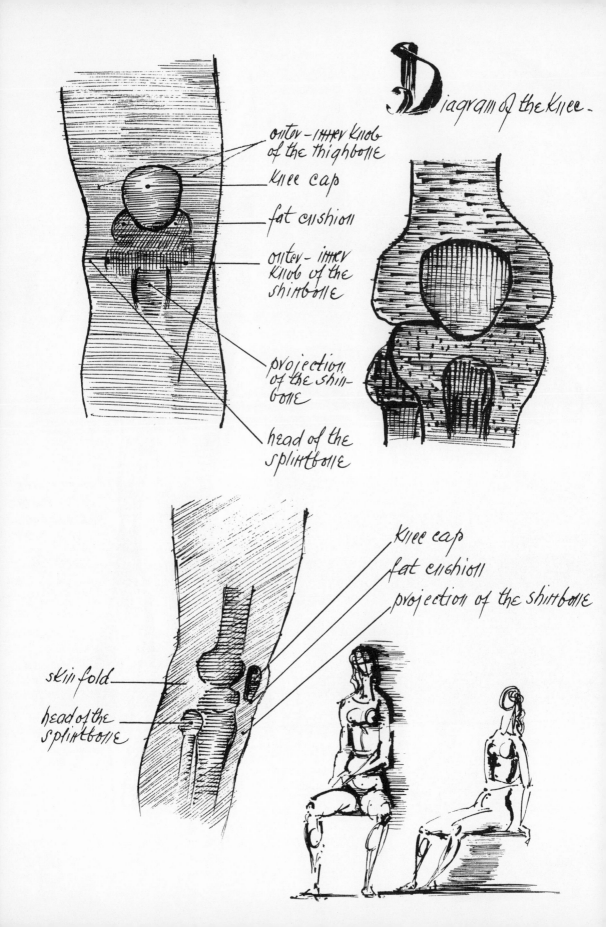

Diagram of the Knee.

outer-inner knob
of the thighbone

Knee cap

fat cushion

outer-inner
knob of the
shinbone

projection
of the shin-
bone

head of the
splintbone

Knee cap
fat cushion
projection of the shintbone

skin fold

head of the
splintbone

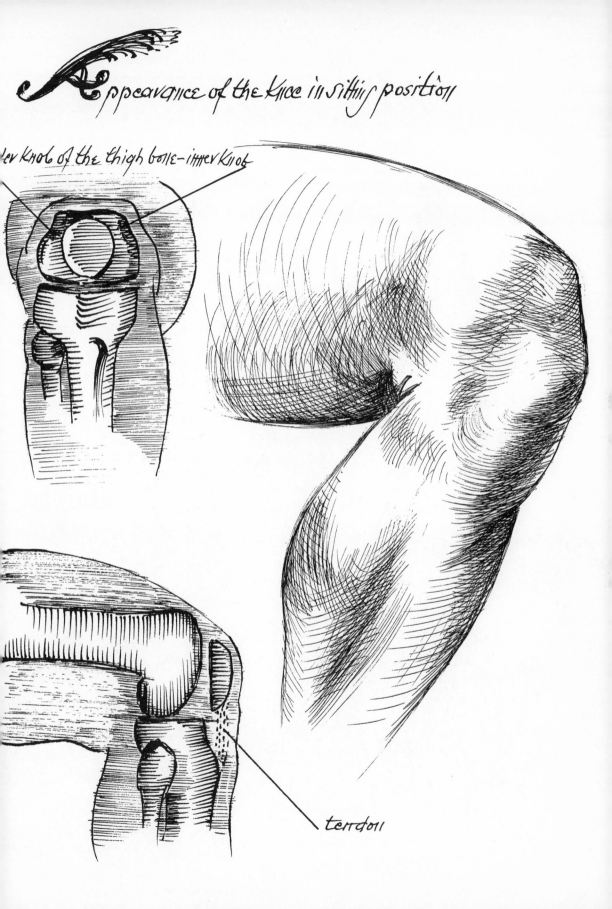

Appearance of the knee in sitting position

ter knob of the thigh bone—inner knob

tendon

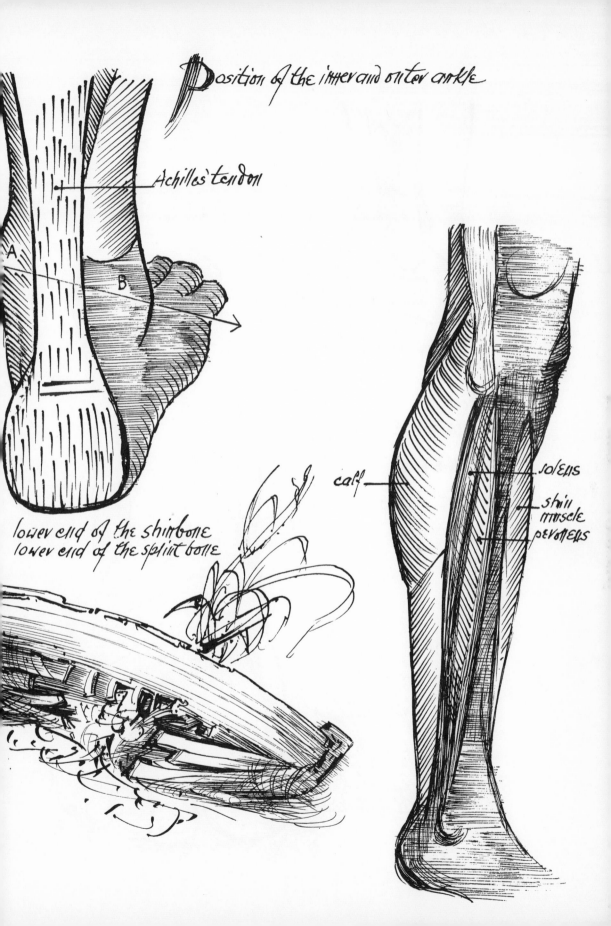

Position of the inner and outer ankle

Achilles` tendon

A

B

lower end of the shinbone
lower end of the splint bone

calf

soleus

shin
muscle
peroneus

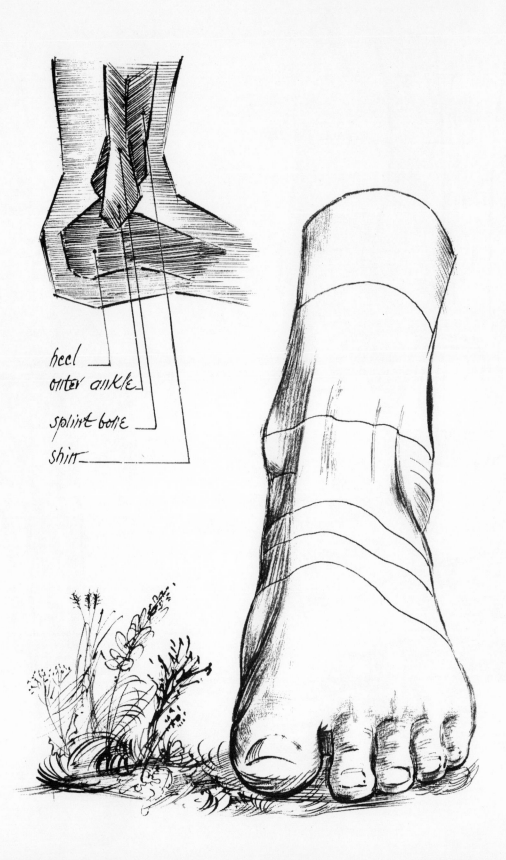

heel

outer ankle

splint bone

shin

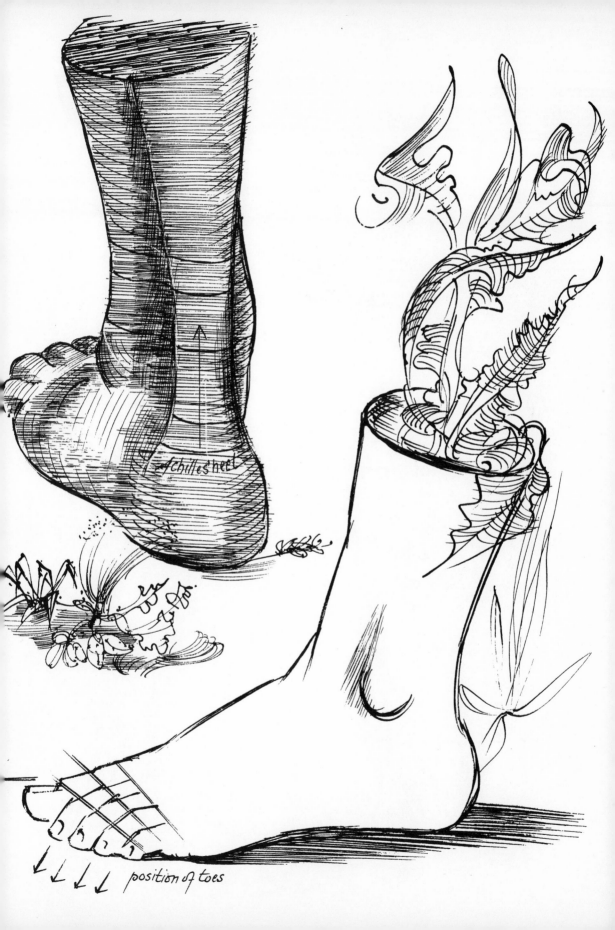

Achilles heel

position of toes

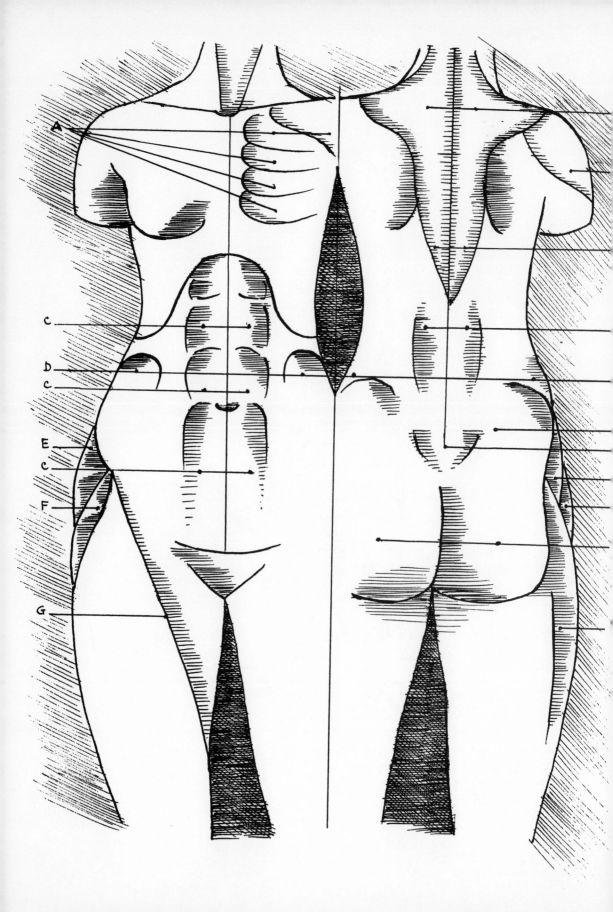

Diagram of the muscles

A breast muscle
B hood muscle
C abdominal
D flank pad
E medial buttock
F tensor

G tailor's muscle
H trapezius
I erector of the spine
J sacroiliac triangle
K buttock
L outer vastus

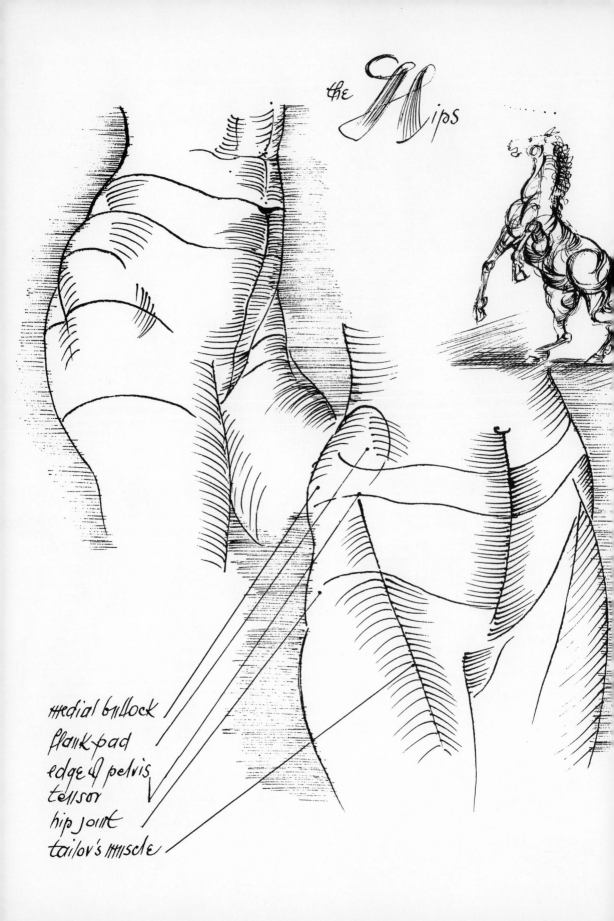

the Hips

medial buttock
flank-pad
edge of pelvis
tensor
hip joint
tailor's muscle

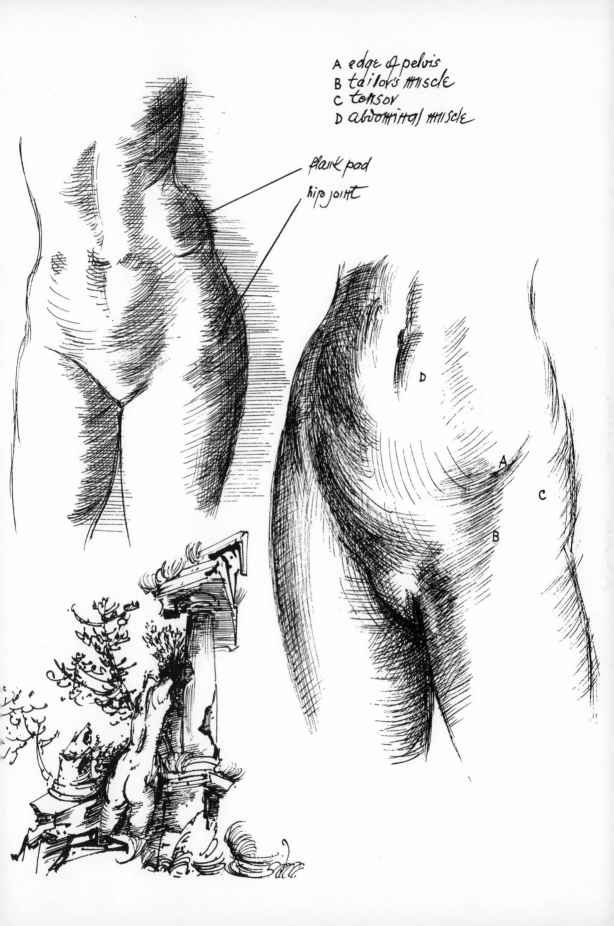

A edge of pelvis
B tailor's muscle
C tensor
D abdominal muscle

flank pad

hip joint

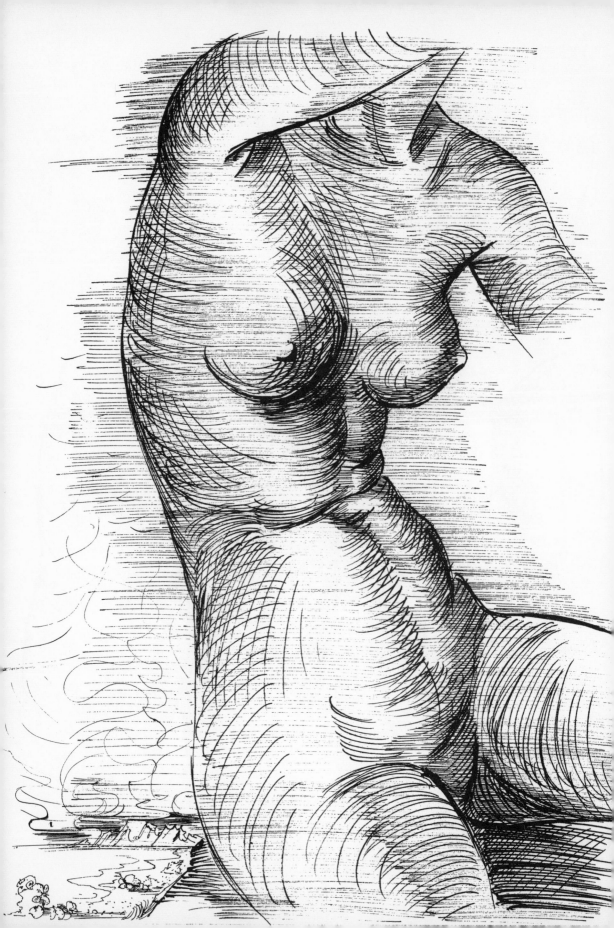

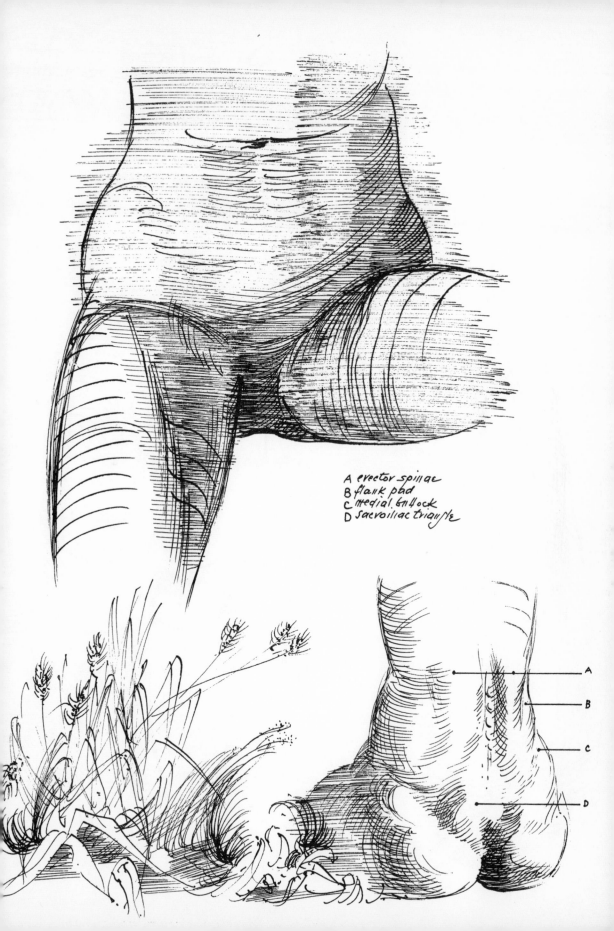

A erector spinae
B flank pad
C medial buttock
D sacroiliac triangle

A
B
C
D

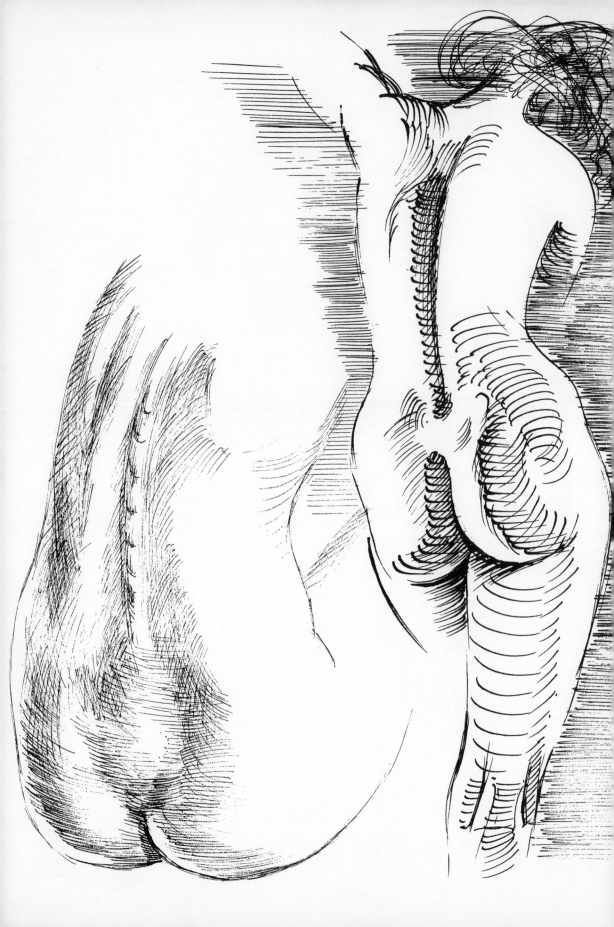

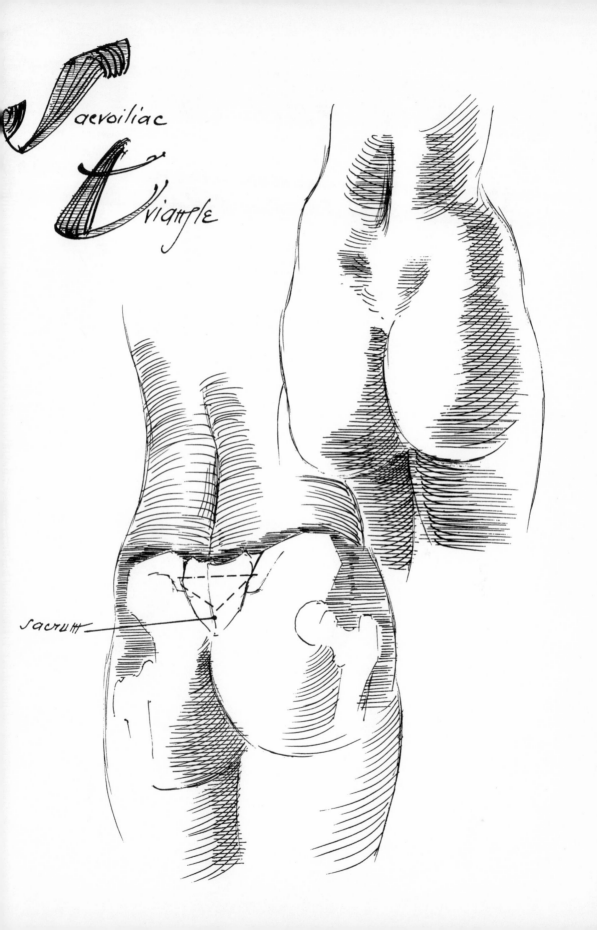

Sacroiliac

Triangle

sacrum

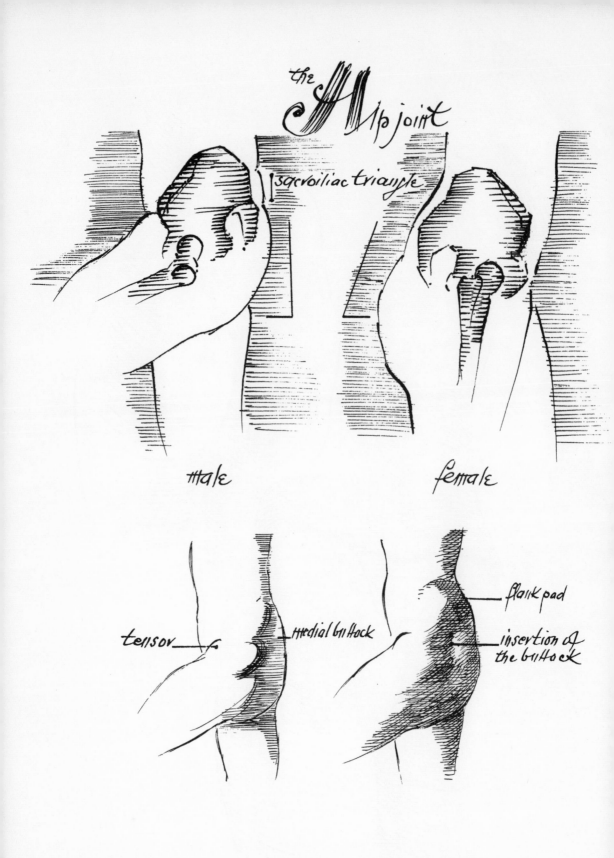

the Hip joint

sacroiliac triangle

male

female

tensor

medial buttock

flank pad

insertion of the buttock

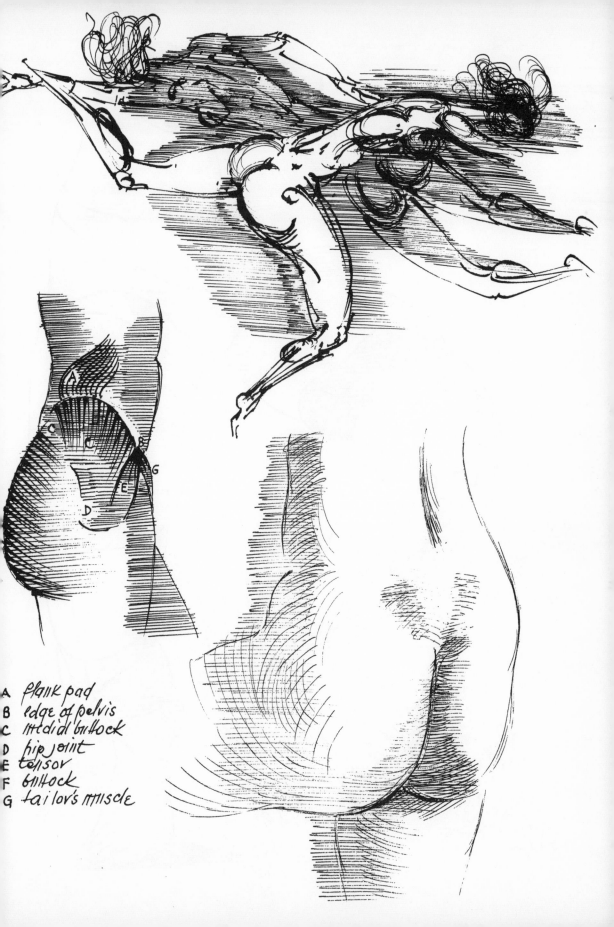

A flank pad
B edge of pelvis
C medial buttock
D hip joint
E tensor
F buttock
G tailor's muscle

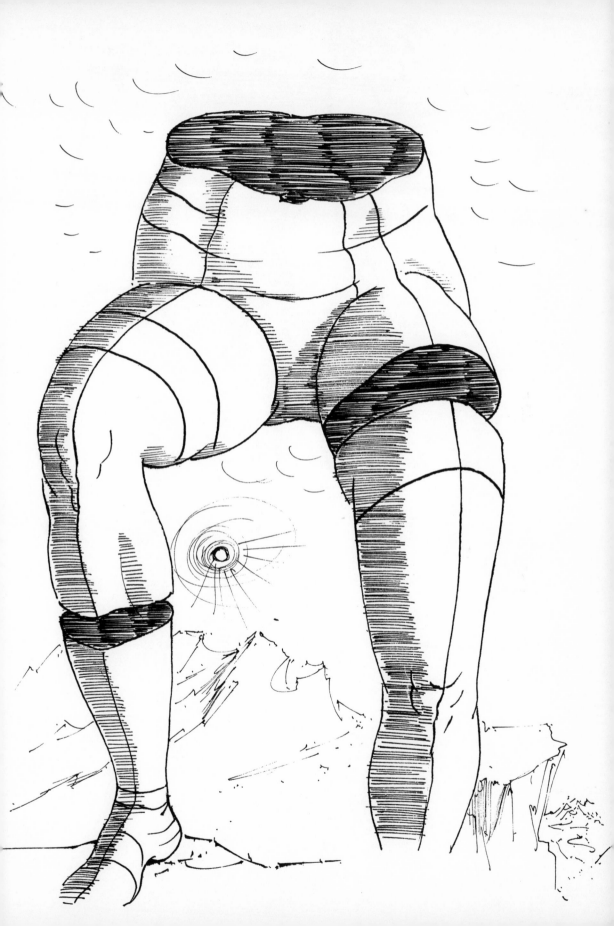

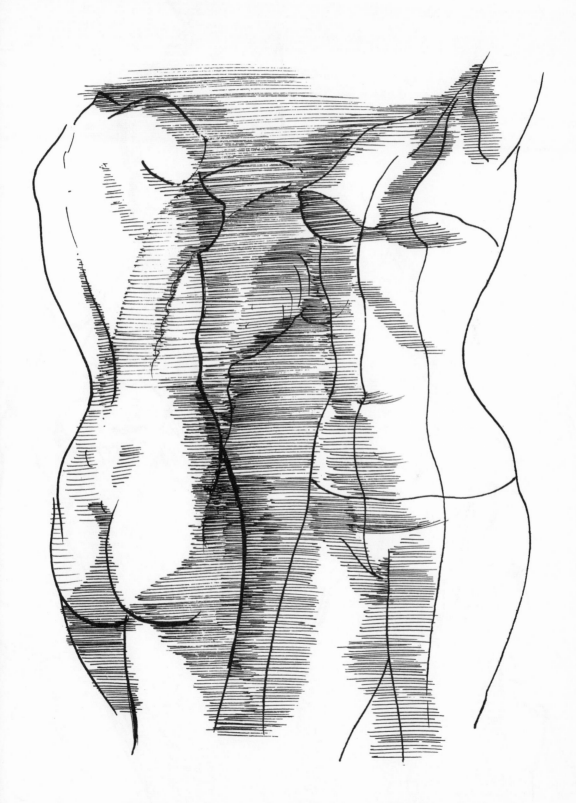

after Myron

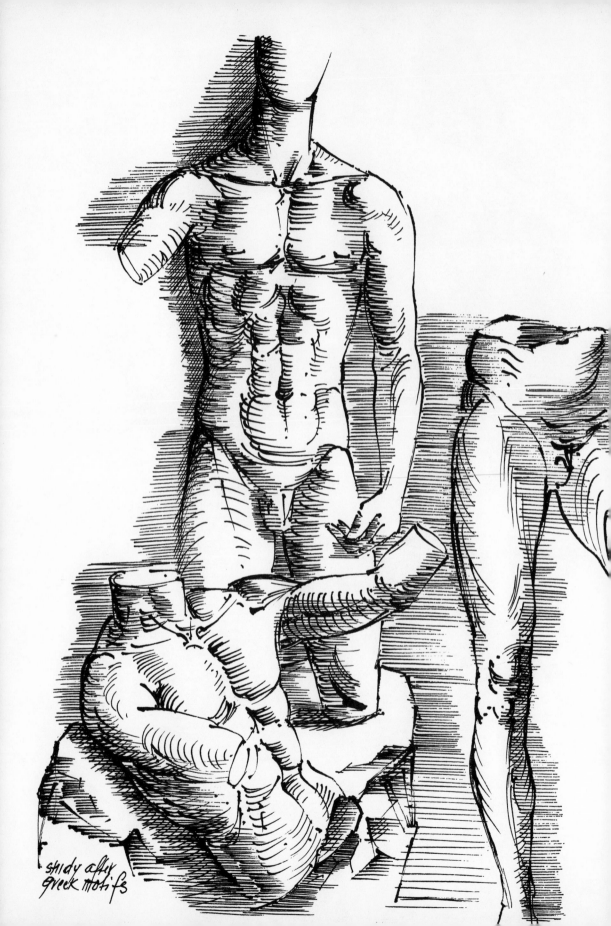

study after
greek motifs

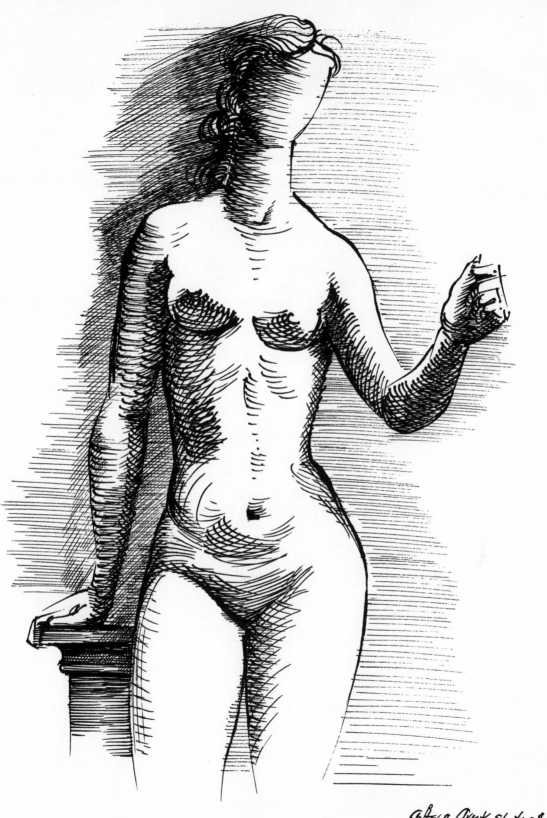

After a Greek statuette

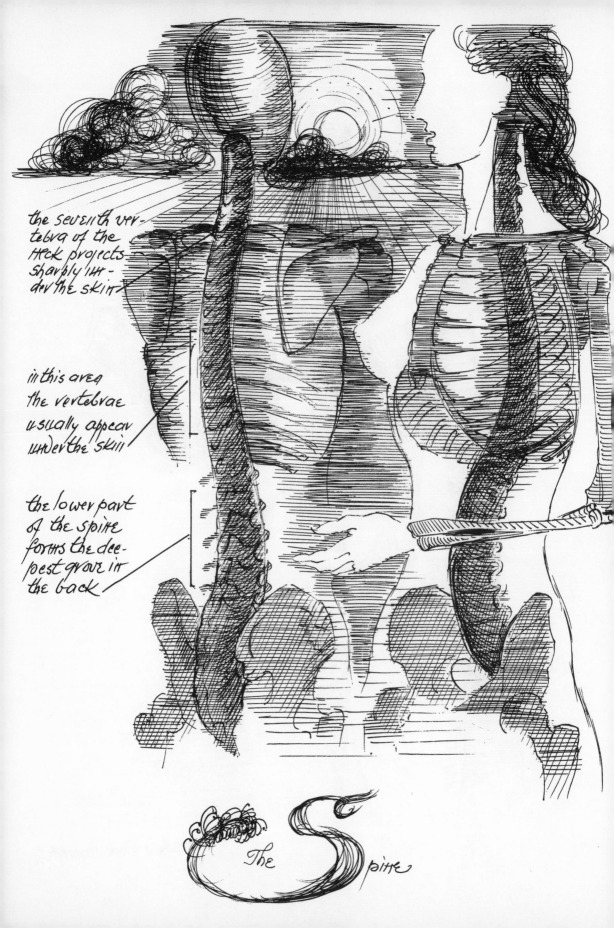

the seventh ver-
tebra of the
neck projects
sharply un-
der the skin

in this area
the vertebrae
usually appear
under the skin

the lower part
of the spine
forms the dee-
pest groove in
the back

The Spine

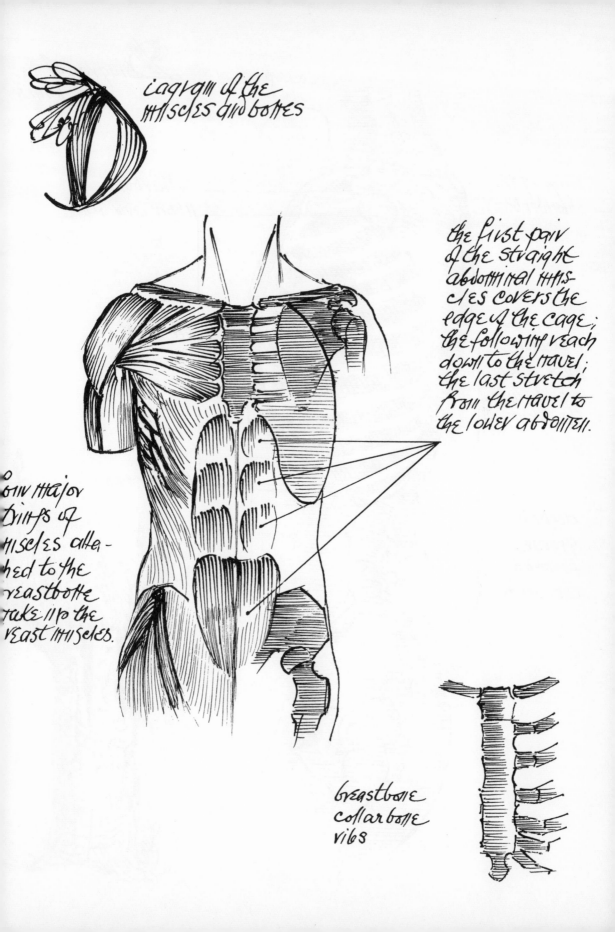

diagram of the
muscles and bones

the first pair
of the straight
abdominal mus-
cles covers the
edge of the cage;
the following reach
down to the navel;
the last stretch
from the navel to
the lower abdomen.

four major
lines of
muscles attac-
hed to the
breastbone
make up the
breast muscles.

breastbone
collarbone
ribs

Diagram of the bones

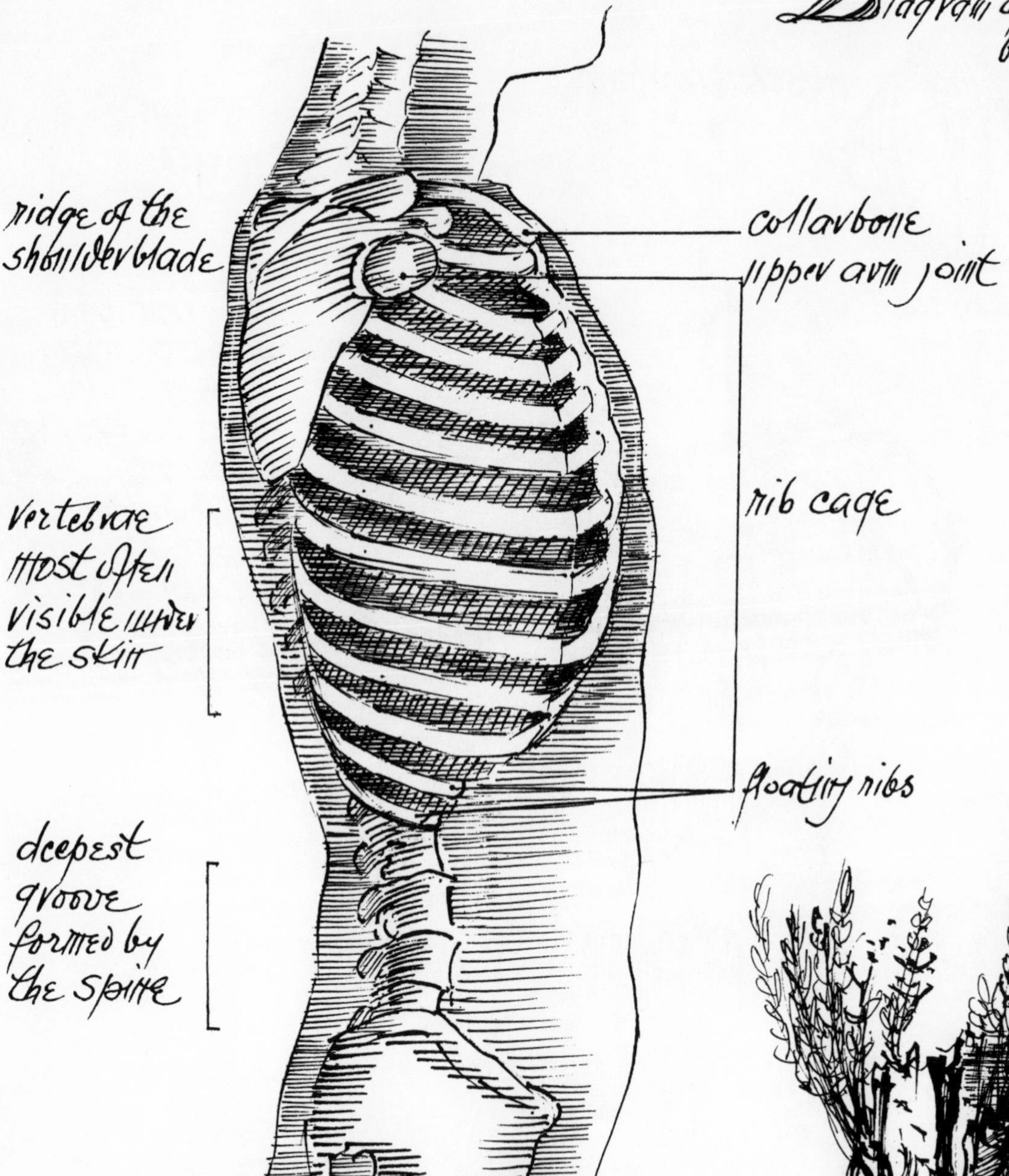

ridge of the shoulderblade
collarbone
upper arm joint
rib cage
vertebrae most often visible under the skin
floating ribs
deepest groove formed by the spine

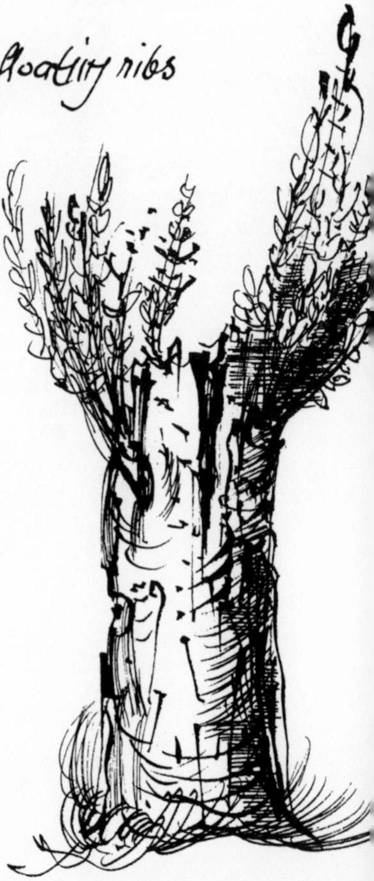

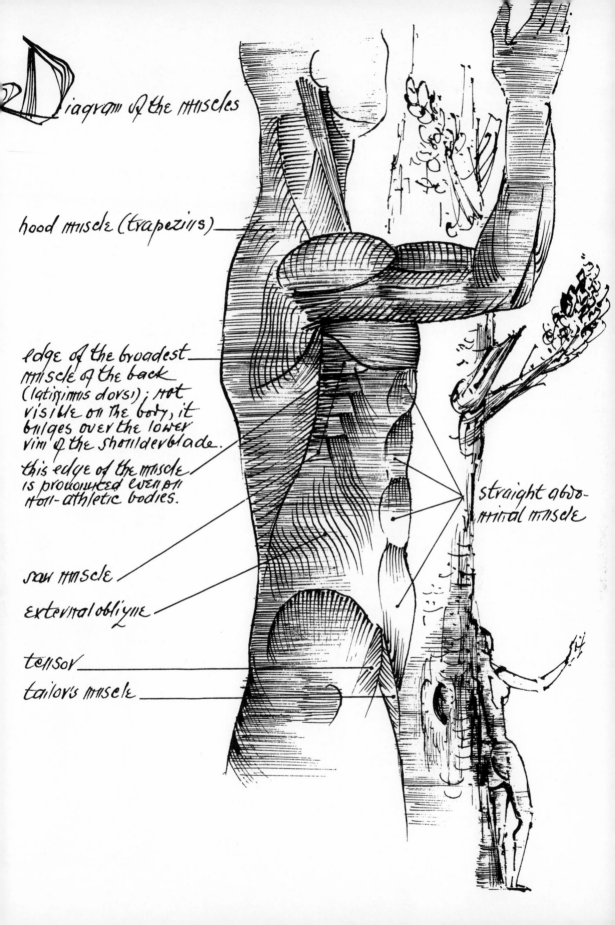

Diagram of the muscles

hood muscle (trapezius)

edge of the broadest
muscle of the back
(latissimus dorsi); not
visible on the body, it
bulges over the lower
rim of the shoulderblade.
this edge of the muscle
is pronounced even on
non-athletic bodies.

saw muscle

external oblique

tensor

tailor's muscle

straight abdo-
minal muscle

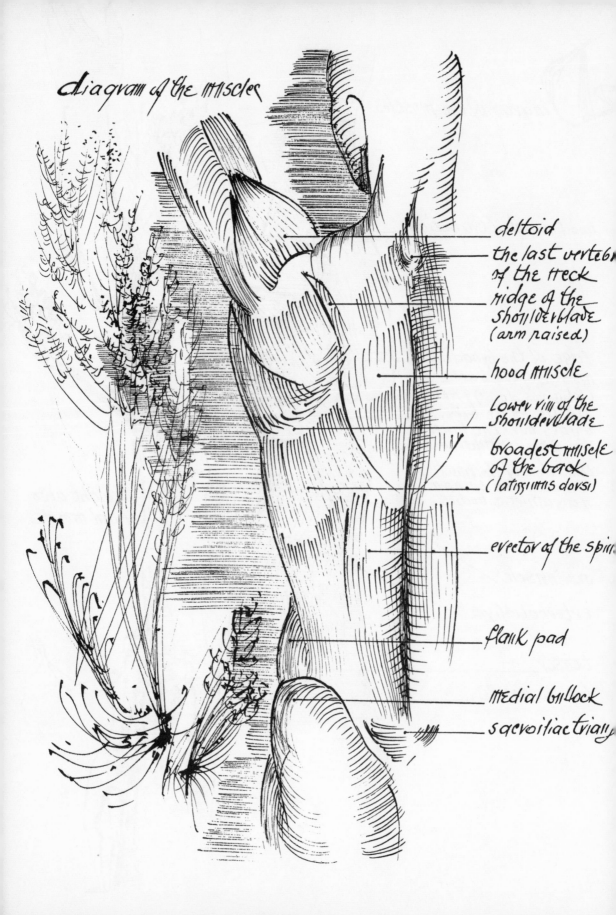

diagram of the muscles

deltoid

the last vertebra
of the neck

ridge of the
shoulderblade
(arm raised)

hood muscle

Lower rim of the
shoulderblade

broadest muscle
of the back
(latissimus dorsi)

erector of the spine

flank pad

medial buttock

sacroiliac triangle

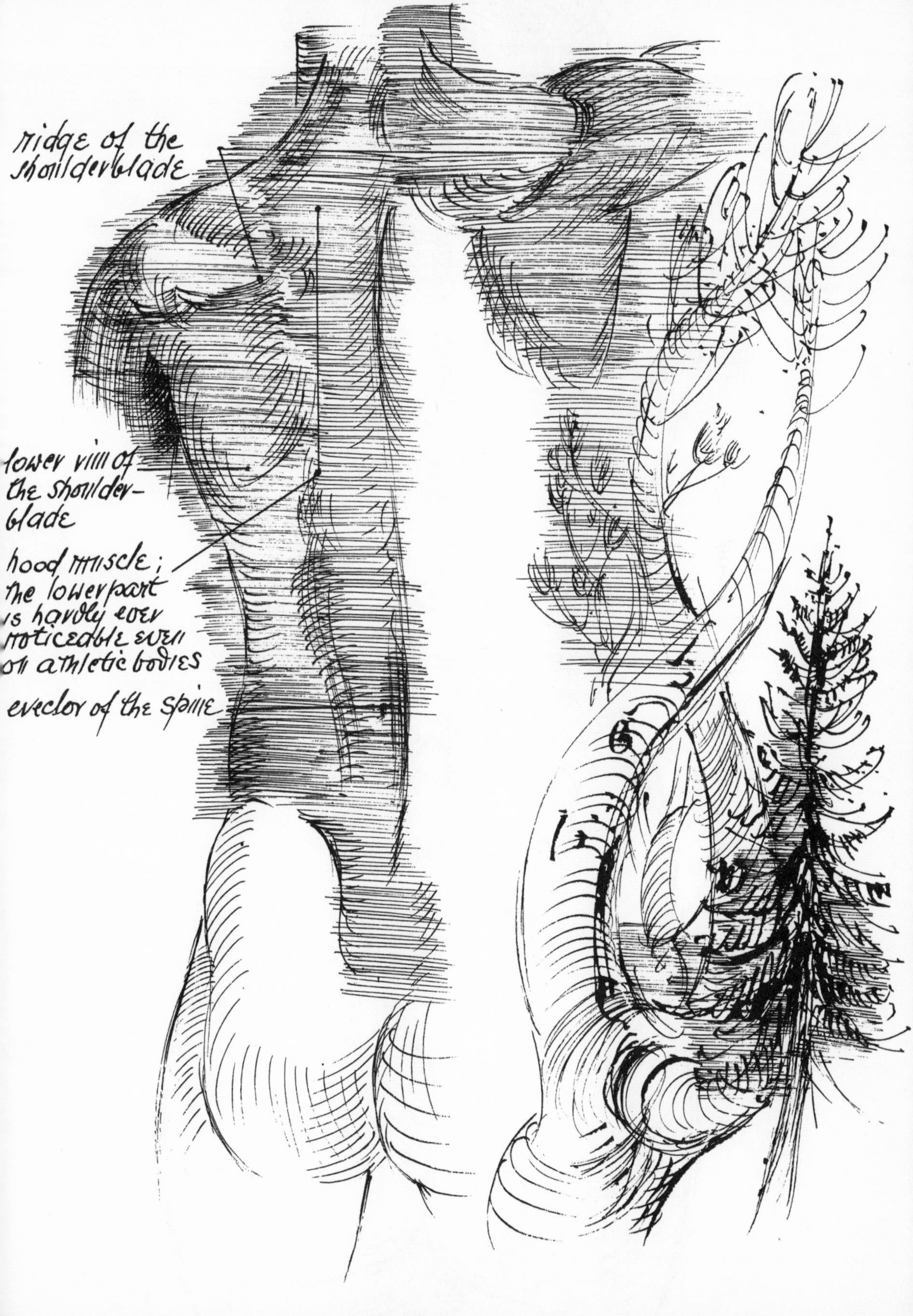

ridge of the
shoulderblade

lower rim of
the shoulder-
blade

hood muscle;
the lower part
is hardly ever
noticeable even
on athletic bodies

erector of the spine

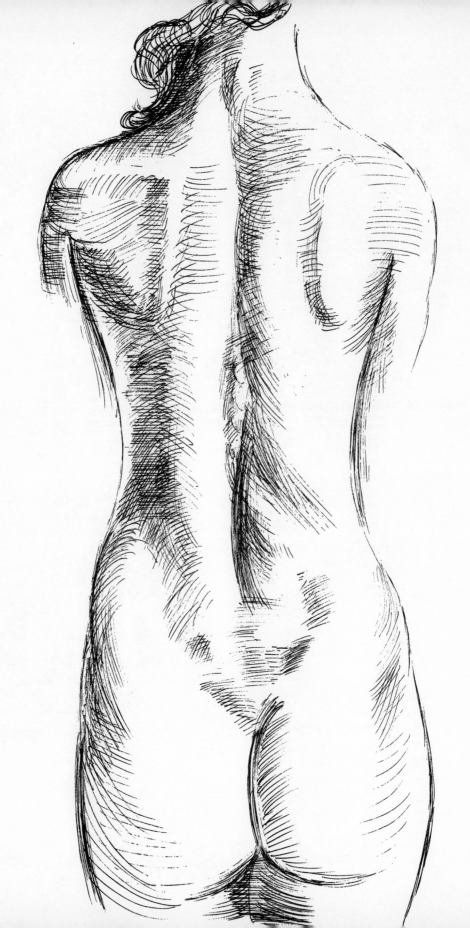

the Figure

athletic body

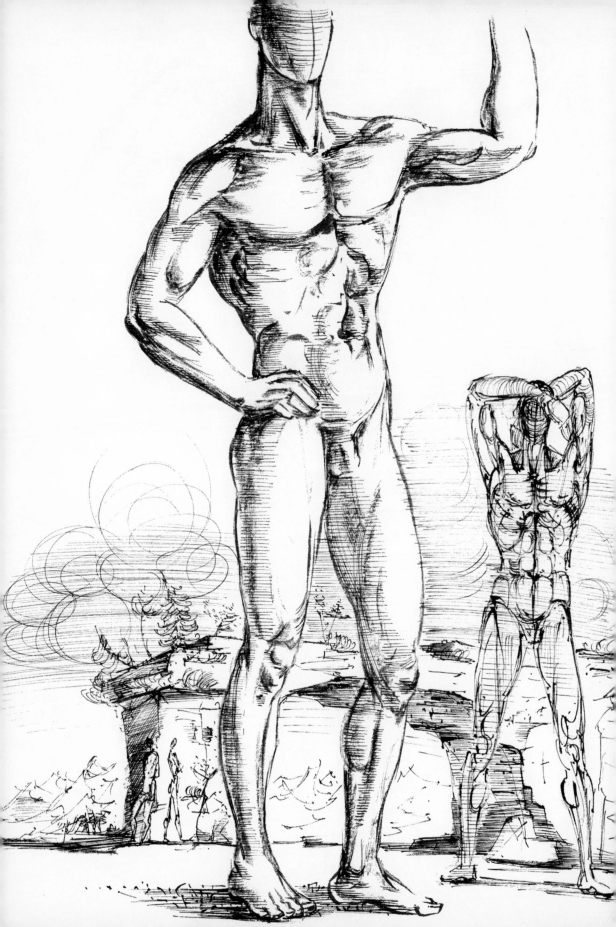

Athletic body

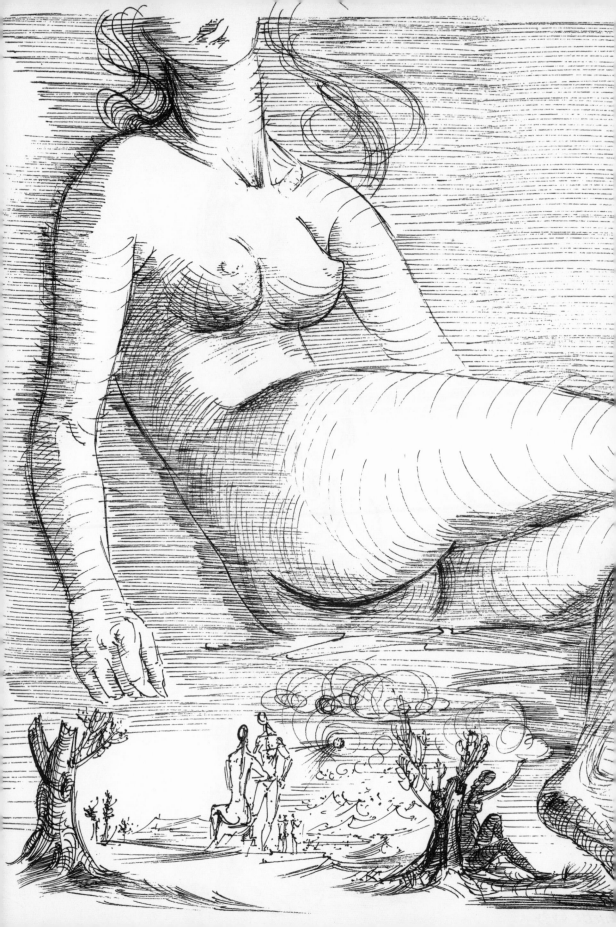

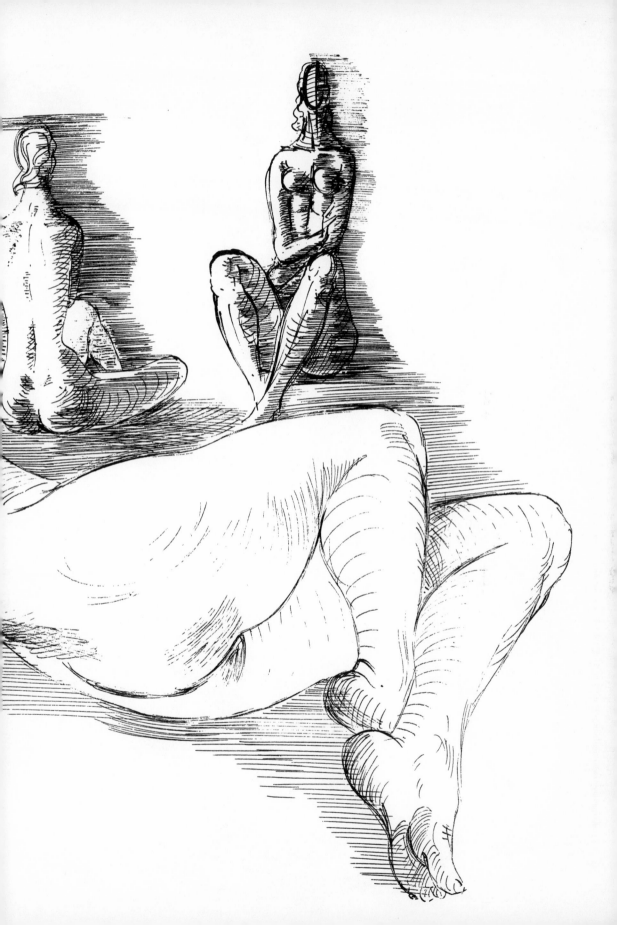

study from an antique figure

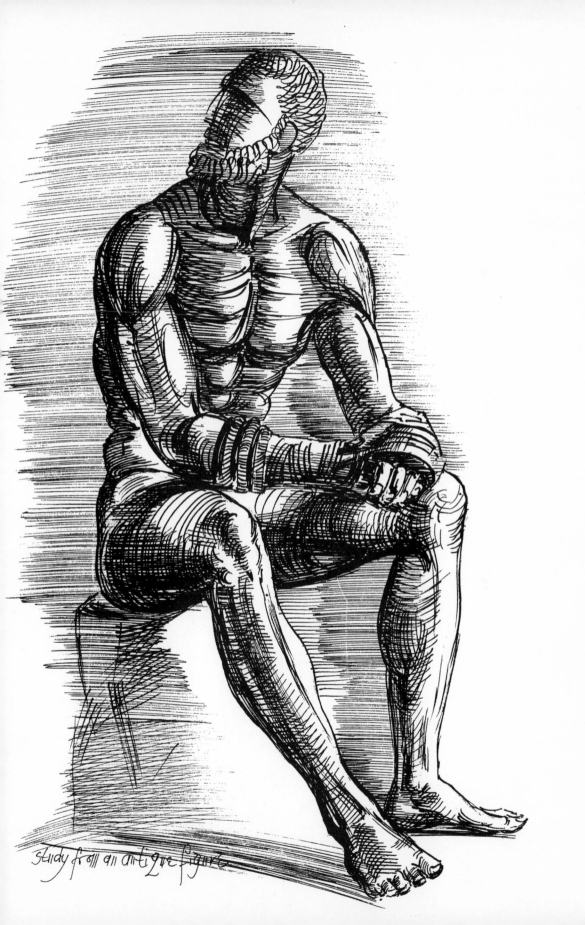

study from an antique figure

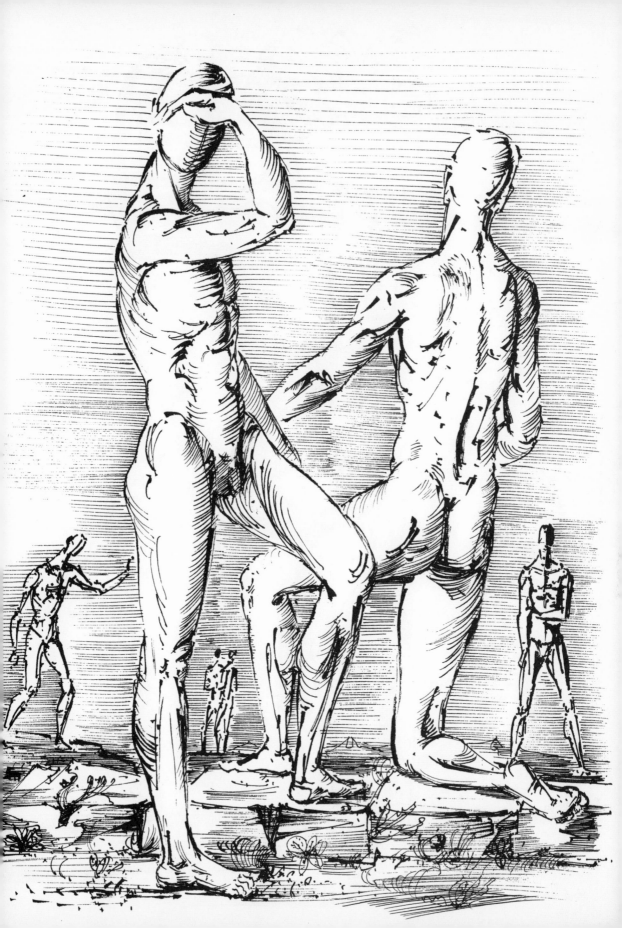

Study from a manikin

Study from a mannikin

study from a manikin

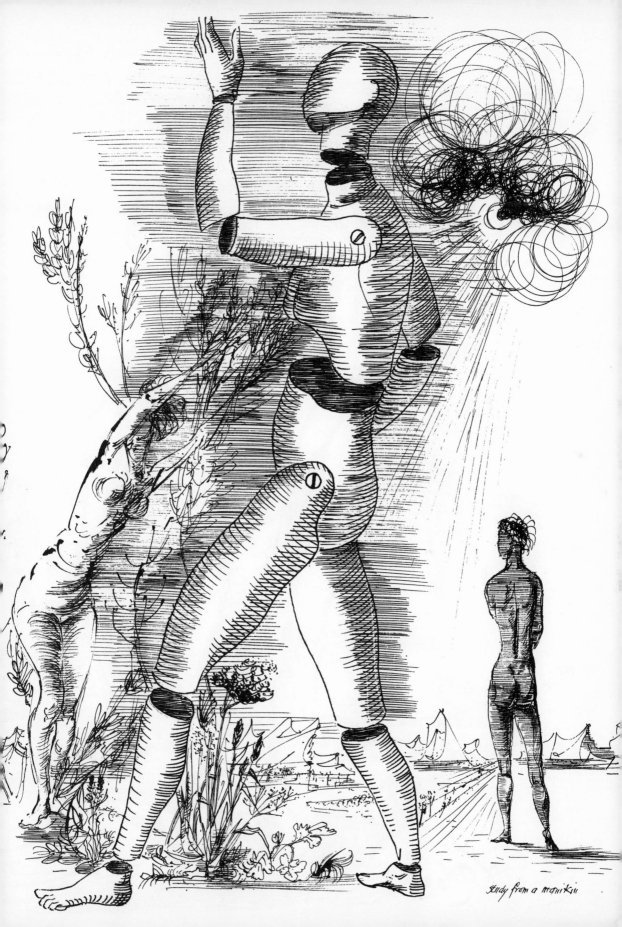

Study from a manikin

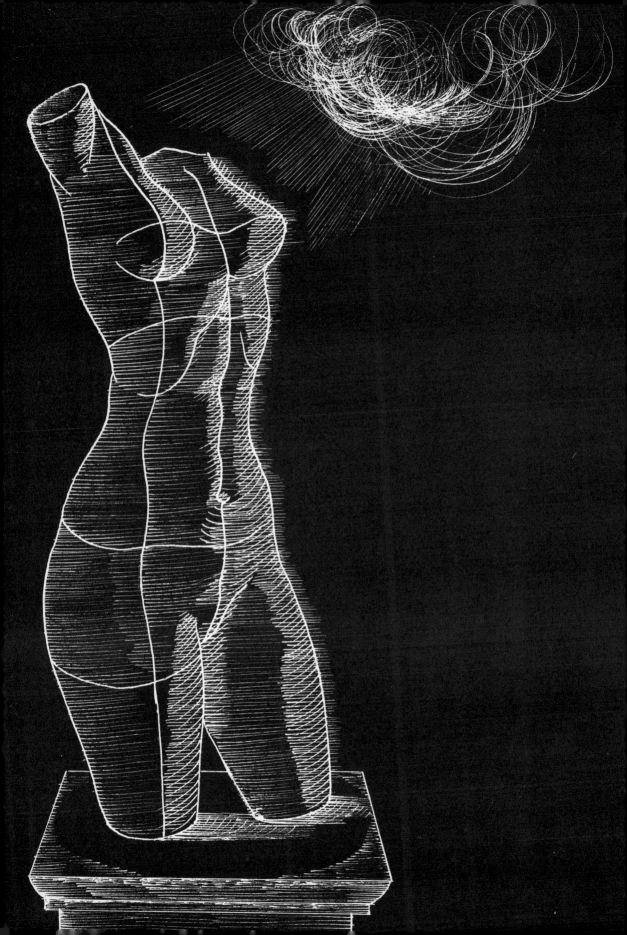